CHRIS NEWTON

A Midsummer
Night Stream

Scenes from an angling life

HOOKED ON BOOKS

amazon.co.uk®

A gift from **Sara**

Happy birthday with all my love From Sara

Gift note included with **A Midsummer Night Stream: Scenes from an angling life**

HOOKED ON BOOKS

2nd Floor, 6-8 Dyer Street, Cirencester, Gloucestershire, GL7 2PF

An imprint of Memoirs Books Ltd. www.mereobooks.com

A Midsummer Night Stream: 978-1-86151-932-0

First published in Great Britain in 2019
by Mereo Books, an imprint of Memoirs Books Ltd.

The address for Memoirs Books Ltd. can be
found at www.mereobooks.com

Memoirs Books Ltd. Reg. No. 7834348

Typeset in 10/15pt Garamond
by Wiltshire Associates Ltd.
Printed and bound in Great Britain

Contents

This book is dedicated to the memory of my late father, Tony Newton, in gratitude for all the times he took me fishing as a boy, and to my late mother Nora for her interest and encouragement, and for teaching me how to cook the catch.

About the author

Chris Newton has been fishing for six decades and writing about it for three. Over the years the focus of his passion has moved from coarse and sea fishing to fly fishing for trout, sea trout and salmon, but he remains at heart an all-round angler and nature lover who is happy to be stationed beside any body of clean water at any season with rod, binoculars and camera. The author of two acclaimed books on fishing-related matters, *Hugh Falkus, A Life On The Edge* and *The Trout's Tale*, and a regular contributor to *Trout and Salmon* and other magazines, he works as an editor and ghostwriter. He describes this entertaining book as 'a little retrospective self-indulgence... a chance to write about my own experiences and my deepest feelings about fishing'.

Introduction

Some years ago, in a jaded moment, I set off for a solo angling holiday in Wales. Its declared purpose was the pursuit of summer sea trout, but the real agenda was the capture not of fish, but of the past. I wanted to try to get swallowed up by the lovely business of fishing as I had been thirty-five years before, as a boy on the banks of the Bridgewater Canal. I had become disillusioned by the superficial quick fix of the day trip, the impossibility of leaving behind the mobile phone, the deadlines and the family responsibilities. I wanted, in short, to take a holiday from being grown up.

I failed, of course. For a day or two, taking a little time off from real life did enable me to concentrate on water and weed and weirpools and to think a little less about my responsibilities back home, but the nagging awareness of the trivial headaches that might be waiting for me in the post, in my email inbox and on the telephone answering machine brought the holiday to a distinctly downbeat end in less than a week. More to the point, I was exhausted. After five days of exploring half the day and fishing most of the night, my back ached, my shoulders were stiff and my hands were scratched and sore. The rear-view mirror of my car revealed eyes of pewter in a mask of stubble. I felt I would never want to cast another fly as long as I lived.

The truth is, *fishing hurts*. The piscatorial Arcadia portrayed in the more romantic fishing books and selectively retained in our own fond memories is very different from the sweaty, gritty, stiff-backed, hollow-eyed ordeal of a twelve-hour day by the river, let alone several of them in succession.

On the drive home I pondered the myth of the carefree schoolboy and reflected that the worries of the average ten-year-old – tedious or impossible schoolwork, parental retribution, peer rejection – are just as daunting at the time, if not more so, than those he will face in later life. And I remembered how often those early outings had ended in despair and anguish because the fish had failed to cooperate, at a time when I could not hope for another appointment with them for weeks, or months.

So I gave up trying to recapture the angling Arcadia which dominates the imagination of every angler with a soul (which is most of us, I hope) – until now. I decided to see if it was possible to capture the flavour of the angling dream in writing while giving an honest account of the reality of the fishing experiences behind it, and to this end I started assembling some stories of my adventures on the river bank, from memory and from my diaries. The stories are all true, subject to a few details that have had to be reconstructed from an incomplete memory, and there is no exaggeration about any of the fish mentioned. The people named are real too, in most cases - I have felt no need to disguise them, as I have (I hope) said nothing likely to upset them.

So here's the book. I hope you like it.

Chris Newton
June 2019

CHAPTER 1

The canal

Two small magicians, each with a jam jar
Cast spells on the water with hazel twig wands…

Ralph McTell, 'Barges'

It was Howard Pemberton's elder brother Brad, standing in the inspection pit in his father's garage torqueing down the cylinder head nuts on the family Vauxhall Cresta with a wrench held between big, oil-blackened hands, who told us about the car that had gone into the Bridgewater Canal. There was a family of four on board, said Brad, Mr and Mrs Harold Longworth and their offspring, Graham and Valerie, and the car had shot off the towpath where it joined the road up past Broadheath and disappeared in a cloud of mud and bubbles, not that anyone was there to see it. It was a spruce green 1955 Ford Prefect, with the chrome side strips and bumper overriders but not the optional heater, according to Brad.

The next day the police located the Prefect and hauled it out with ropes, but of the Longworth family, said Brad, there had been no trace.

"You 'ave to watch your brakes with them Fords" he said. "Never 'appen with this. Ten-inch drums. Stop on a sixpence," and he went back to wrenching.

For the rest of that summer of 1960 I fished in fear, imagining each time my line caught on a snag that I had hooked Mr or Mrs Longworth, or perhaps Graham or Valerie, and that my next heave on the line would bring a grinning cadaver lurching to the surface. I could find nothing about the tragedy in the *Sale and Stretford Guardian*, but Brad could explain that; it had all been hushed up to protect Ford's sales figures.

Certainly there *were* bodies in the canal – those of domestic animals, usually, of the kind you'd expect from a watercourse which served several of the denser suburbs of south Manchester as an informal refuse disposal system; cats and mongrels, ducks and hens (people kept poultry then for the eggs, rather than as a statement of harmony with Gaia) and homing pigeons that hadn't.

One year we had an Airedale. It drifted up and down between Timperley Bridge and the station right through the school holidays, sidling into our swims every so often to allow us to monitor its progress from cherished ex-pet to bleached, disintegrating blob.

That's canals for you, squatting at your feet, oily and silent, waiting, watching and occasionally giving you a nasty turn, just to make sure you don't start taking them for granted. I never liked to picture the squalor of the canal bed, particularly after the tale of the Longworths. No doubt there was all manner of esoteric refuse; tin cans, typewriters, footwear, the jettisoned hauls of burglars, unexploded bombs.

The barrier between the bright world above and the unseen one beneath was breached only by our lines and hooks. Though the water was dirty, it was by no means poisonous. To the repeated astonishment of non-fishing adults, it held plenty of fish – roach, perch, silver bream, occasionally even a stray tench to set our hearts racing.

Over the course of half a dozen seasons in the late 1950s and early sixties I got to know those fish very well. The canal was three miles from home or (once I was allowed to go under my own steam) about fifteen minutes by push-bike. I fished it for the first time on an August day in 1958, when I was eight. Brian Cowburn's father had offered to take Brian, Michael Rogers, John Finlay and me fishing; real fishing, with rods. I was already nurturing an interest in proper angling because I had reached the age when paddling about in Baguley Brook (Paddly Brook, we called it) in shorts and wellingtons with a shrimping net had begun to make me feel self-conscious. I knew of older boys who did their fishing with rods and lines in real rivers and lakes, and felt I should be joining them. We didn't have any rivers or lakes to speak of within a boy's range of home, but we did have the Bridgewater Canal.

The afternoon began with an unbargained-for wait in John Finlay's kitchen while his mother forced him to do the washing-up, an act of cruelty I had never imagined possible. I remember sitting at the green Formica kitchen table, my heart going out to John as his tears of desperation mingled with the suds.

When we eventually got to the canal, I assembled my home-made rig, which was a 5ft garden cane, painted with bands of blue to simulate whippings, and an old wooden Nottingham reel given to me by Great Uncle Alec and lashed on with string. The reel would turn only when great force was applied to its rim, but because I knew nothing of reels I concluded that this was how Nottingham reels were designed and that you had to wind the line on and off by hand; I did not realise that it had seized up and was all but useless. I had loaded the reel with string and to the end of the string I had knotted a length of 4lb 'Luron 2' nylon monofilament (the pun in the name did not occur to me until many years later). For the business end I had a red-tipped porcupine-quill float, some split shot and a packet of eyed hooks, bought from Haslam's hardware shop in Washway Road with my father that morning. This was all the tackle I owned. For bait, we had worms in jam-jars – what else?

It was hot and sunny as we tackled up on the cindered towpath. The others had boys' fishing outfits – miniature glass-fibre spinning rods with tiny, useless, fixed-spool reels – except for Brian Cowburn, who was using a rod made for him by his father from a tank aerial. In those days, not much more than a decade after the war, tank aerials were thought to be just the job for a low-budget boy's rod. I tried Brian's and found it absurdly heavy and floppy compared to my rigid cane, but as Mr Cowburn was there I praised it politely.

Every fifteen yards or so, openings had been cut in the reeds to allow access to the water. Most of these bays were occupied by grown-up anglers on baskets, so we trampled out openings in places which were not really fishing spots and swung our tackle out over the reeds. When we trod on the reeds, they produced a sweet garden-pea fragrance; even now, when I smell crushed reeds, I am back beside that canal. We could hardly cast at all, but that didn't worry us – the water looked deep enough to hold anything you wanted it to, right up to the edge. Compared to Paddly Brook, it was the Marianas Trench.

It took me a while to get my float to cock properly, like the pictures I had seen in books, but almost as soon as it had done so it went under. Is there a god of young anglers? He was certainly on duty that day. I pulled back, and up flew a perch – bright, stripy, spikey, beautiful and bigger than anything I had caught from the brook, even the six-inch stone loach that had lived for a year in an old washbasin with just some stones stolen from Mr Barlow's rockery for company. It was exactly the way things are supposed to happen, and as you can see, I have never forgotten it.

We were there for perhaps an hour and a half, and I caught seven more perch, all the same size as the first. I'm pretty sure no one else had as many; Brian Cowburn, in fact, put in a complaint to his father because I had caught more than he had. On Mr Cowburn's instructions, we put most of the perch back, though I defied him by bashing one over the head so that I could show it to my parents.

I couldn't wait to go again. For the rest of that summer and throughout the next, I besieged my father with weekly demands for further visits. Most of them were granted; thanks, Dad.

After a while Dad started leaving me to fish while he and my brother and sister went off to do the shopping. Within a season or so, my parents found the pressure to allow me to go on my own unbearable, and relented. So from the age of ten, still in short trousers, I was cycle-borne and free. I began to fish the canal pretty much whenever I wanted to.

The idyll continued through my twelfth and thirteenth summers. From Sale Library I borrowed books by the gods of the game, men like Richard Walker, Fred J Taylor, Bernard Venables, BB and Maurice Wiggin, and learned everything I could about fishing. Or at least, about fishing as it was practised in the great waters of the south of England; there were many references to broads, fens, drains, chalkstreams and gravel pits. I pored over my father's Ordnance Survey maps for evidence that a fen or a chalkstream might be found within a Sunday afternoon drive of Sale, without success. We had drains all right, but not the kind people went fishing in.

After a season or two I acquired a proper rod, 11ft long and made of whole cane with a glass-fibre tip. It was a dreadful thing by later standards, heavy, floppy and fragile, but it was a proper working rod, with rings and a reel seat. With its help, in due course, I caught many roach and silver bream. But for a long time, no more perch; years later I read that a ghostly disease had ravaged Britain's perch population in the late fifties, so I must have squeezed in my angling début just in time.

I got to know some of the other anglers. Most of them were older, much older; middle-aged, unhappy-looking men, weekend fishers who would come stomping past in ones and twos when the sun was well over the yardarm, laden with huge baskets and boxes and nets, to set up camp for a day away from the missus or the factory (it was from these men that I first learned that there are other reasons for going fishing than to catch fish). Despite the extra walking required, they seemed to prefer the deeper water further up towards Brooklands, which left the shallows by Timperley Bridge to me and the other boys. The quest for depth would seize me in due course as it does all young anglers, and many older ones – what a false god it is! – before enlightenment dawned.

These men peppered the water with multi-coloured maggots and Spratts Silvercloud groundbait and sat hunched over long roach poles made of glass fibre or Spanish reed. Sometimes they got the fish to co-operate, at least the small ones, and filled their nets with silver roach and skimmers; more often, they caught little or nothing. On these occasions, they simply grumbled and blamed it on the fish.

To me, it was obvious why they were so unsuccessful. They were all coming down at the same time, and far too late at that. On crowded summer Sundays the bites invariably stopped soon after breakfast. How had they not discovered this, and learned to creep out on a weekday dawn as I did?

My library books revealed a few other things these men did not seem to know. One was that you don't have to use maggots for roach – in fact on heavily-fished waters you should avoid them. When I read that bread paste was a good bait for the big ones, I filched some bread from the bread-bin, concealed it in my bedside cupboard for a few days until it was stale, soaked and mashed it as described in the book, squeezed the water out through a cloth and took it to the canal for an evening session.

I picked a spot away from the grown-ups, along a reed-lined stretch near the bridge which the other anglers always dismissed as too shallow and too near the road and the station for fishing. I threw a few loose pieces of the paste in and waited. When the water was calm along this part of the canal, as it usually was, the surface was criss-crossed by the reflections of the semi-detached houses opposite. You could chart the progress of your float through your swim with great precision as it slid at the pace of the minute hand of a grandfather clock along the tiles, past the chimney stack, across the guttering and out into the grey space that led to the next roof.

Several times the float completed its slow creep past the tiles and chimneys undisturbed, but then, just as I was beginning to run out of patience and thinking about reverting to maggots, it went decisively under. A few seconds later I found myself netting a thumping roach, twice the size of the usual run; ten ounces or more. I put it in the keepnet, jubilant, feeling like the cleverest angler in England. I caught another, and another. By the time the sun had set and the air was turning chill, I had taken seven cracking roach, all between half a pound and three quarters of a pound in weight. They weren't just bigger than usual, they were in better condition, without a torn lip or a frayed fin between them; these were the older roach, the ones that had learned to disdain the maggots which had tempted them in youth and had consequently been enjoying a life free from the trauma of capture – until now, of course.

I decided to keep this discovery to myself. I thought that if I told the other anglers about it, they would soon all be using bread and it would lose its magic. But after a couple of outings, the bites stopped coming so freely. I had discovered how quickly fish learn. So I moved on to cheese, particularly attractive, said the book, to chub; perhaps there were some in the canal, all unsuspected (and unsuspecting) because no one had ever used the right bait. I scaled up to a size 6 hook as instructed by Dick Walker in *No Need to Lie*, four sizes bigger than anything the regulars would dream of using, and moulded pieces of Cracker Barrel mild cheddar on to it. I did not catch any chub, but I did win the roach back for a while.

The next summer I got interested in hempseed. I had read many references to this arcane substance, so deadly a bait for roach that it had apparently been banned on many waters. I had no idea whether it was allowed in Cheshire, or if those in authority gave a damn how we did our fishing up north for that matter, but I had certainly never heard of anyone actually using it.

I found a packet in Bailey's tackle shop in Regent Street, Altrincham; I remember that it came from Holland and bore the name J P Sluis. I boiled the seeds in a milk pan when my mother was out shopping until the white insides were showing, as instructed in the book. The smell was pungent, yeasty and sickly. I think I got into a bit of trouble over it when she came home.

On the Saturday, the rest of the family were going out for the day. As was customary by now, I wasn't going with them. I had more important things to do.

I set up the usual float tackle and started to go through the motions with maggots, but every twenty minutes or so I would look around to check that no one was watching, walk a few yards to the right and toss in a handful of hempseed. Then I would press a grain on to a size 18 hook-to-nylon and cast out for a few minutes to see if anything was happening. For a long time, it wasn't.

I think it was about midday when the action started. I noticed that the surface around the place where the hempseed had gone in had started to stir and shimmer in that thrilling way that speaks of fish. I cast, and the float shot under with incredible speed, much faster than I had ever seen it move before, and of course I struck and hit thin air. I missed a lot more bites before I realised that I was over-exciting the fish. Throwing a dozen grains in at a time might coax a hittable bite, but a handful would send them berserk.

By evening I had caught twenty-three roach, all of which weighed over half a pound and the largest 1lb 4oz. It was the biggest roach I had ever seen anywhere except Tatton Mere, but that's a story for a later chapter.

Around six o'clock, with my deadline approaching and sport fading, I noticed two middle-aged anglers approaching on their homeward trudge, both laden like mules, sweaty, grunting and flushed, though not, I guessed, with success. I lifted the net ostentatiously (and not without difficulty) out of the water as if I had just happened to choose that moment to start packing up. The fish on top flapped weakly in the evening sunshine. I dug up the biggest roach and made sure it was in view.

"Bloody hell!" said the first man. "You were int' right spot then."

"Caught them on hempseed," I said, swollen with pride.

"Bloody little liar" said the man. You just 'appened on t' shoal. We've been after them bastards all day."

"No, hempseed, look," I said. "Dutch, you know." I showed them the baitbox, which had a few damp grains still sticking to it. They peered, exclaimed, exchanged glances.

"That's banned, that is," said the second man. "Alan Vaughan catches you, that's you off t' water for good." Alan Vaughan was the bailiff; he lived opposite.

"And yer tackle taken off yer," said the first man.

"And up in front o' t' magistrates," said the second.

"Oh it's perfectly legal!" I protested, though I could feel my face reddening. "It's only banned on the South Forty Foot and Hickling Broad, and, er, the Great Ouse." I pronounced it "Owze". These places were just names to me; borrowed icons of coarse angling, collected from my library reading. But I dropped them without conviction. Of course, the men were right. My wonderful day had all been too good to be true; I had broken the law. I was lucky not to be down at the station now, submitting to the inking of my fingertips and looking at several years in Borstal.

The men marched on, leaving the question of whether I was to be reported agonisingly open.

So it was guilt, and the fear of jail, that stopped me from using hempseed again, at least for a while. Later I discovered it was perfectly legal on the canal; it had never occurred to anyone to ban it.

One Saturday morning I arrived at my favourite spot by the footbridge to find a newcomer in my place, a slight youth about the same age as myself. He was using a Spanish reed match rod, tipped with built cane and fully fourteen feet long, and he was sitting on a tackle basket at least twice the size of my junior model. To either side of him were boxes of coloured maggots and casters and buckets of groundbait, just like the grown-up anglers.

His name was Pete Nelson, and he turned out to be the first angler I'd met who looked as if he might be able to teach me a thing or two. Pete's house in Sylvan Avenue backed on to the canal from the other side of the railway, so he could, if he'd wanted to, have chucked in his groundbait from the bottom of the garden before setting off; and Pete knew all about groundbait. He demonstrated how to work a shoal of roach or bream into a feeding frenzy with a cloud of ground bread and particle baits, as they are called now; no need for hempseed. He used very small hooks, size 18 or 20, with single maggots, chrysalis (we hadn't yet learned to call them casters) or punched bread. He did canal fishing the way the grown-ups did it, but better; he would start earlier, read the signs, change tactics until he found the fish.

My philosophy was rooted in the natural approach, thanks to Walker & co – big baits on big hooks, throw out a few samples and wait. Good for singling out the big fish, not so clever where there aren't any. In those days we were certain there were *always* big fish, just waiting to be caught, not discovering until much later that this was not quite true.

Pete was 13 like me, but he dressed 16. I remember him always in black, well before it became the classless fashion colour it remains today; a black leather jacket or waistcoat over a white shirt, black jeans with turnups, black winkle-pickers, while I was still in sandals and hand-knitted Fairisle pullovers. Even his fishing basket was painted black, the paint a handy dodge to keep the wickerwork rigid. Pete was James Dean to my Julian from the Famous Five, though facially he looked quite a lot like Allan Clarke from the Hollies, who were becoming very big then and like us were from the Manchester area. When I got to know him a little better I pointed this out to him, but someone had already told him, a girl I think.

For two seasons we fished together, not just by Timperley Bridge but further up around Dunham and Broadheath and sometimes on more distant waters like Lymm Dam, Irlam Old River and the River Dane. We got there on our bikes, of course, our baskets cutting into our shoulders, rods and bank-sticks tied to our cross-bars. For these outings, we would meet up at dawn at the railway bridge on Carrington Moss, a couple of miles out from home.

At first Pete was as enthusiastic about these expeditions as I was, but some time during our third summer, by which time we must both have been fifteen, I sensed that his appetite was flagging. Once I had to cycle all the way to his house to rouse him from Sunday morning slumber; we both had parental carte blanche to spend the whole day by the hallowed waters of Lymm Dam, but he had found it impossible to leave his bed and did not seem too pleased to find me banging on his door.

On the day of the big fish, I knew I'd be starting without him. He was going out the previous evening, he had said, and an early night would be difficult. He said I should come too, to meet some friends of his down at the new bowling alley in Broadheath. But I didn't know how to go to a bowling alley, what to wear or what to say to the friends. There was also a practical problem – I didn't have a part-time job like Pete, who helped his dad with his window-cleaning business, so I had no money other than my five shillings a week pocket money, which usually went on sweets, maggots, airgun slugs and Corona limeade.

I said I would bait up a second swim next to mine, so that he would find the fish waiting for him when he got there. I tried to get him to promise to be there by nine, but he said he couldn't be sure just when it would be.

It turned out a warm, overcast day, perfect for fishing,

and I felt sure Pete would be there beside me straight after breakfast, whacking into the roach with the fourteen-footer, racing me for the biggest bag. We always did that; I wouldn't like to say who won more often, though it was probably Pete. I kept glancing along the towpath, watching for the familiar slight figure in black, rod in hand, basket slung from shoulder, but the more I looked, the more he didn't come.

I chucked in the groundbait, handful after handful, some for Pete, some for me, and I started catching roach, then small bream. It was all going so well – what a day for Pete to go missing.

And then the float went under in a more conclusive way than usual and I lifted the rod and immediately knew what angling writers meant when they talked about striking into a brick wall.

I had caught a lot of fish by then, including a bream of almost two pounds, but all of them, when you pulled, had answered the helm and started to give ground. This one just kept boring away from me along the bottom. It actually took line from the reel, an unprecedented liberty and something I had previously only read about. I resisted as firmly as I dared; my left leg began to shake (it still does sometimes when I get a big fish on). I had to pull so hard I felt sure the hook length would break, but it didn't, and at last in came the fish and I pushed the net under it and hauled it onto the grass.

I recognised it immediately from the literature as a mirror carp; a leviathan, a fantastic, fabulous, undreamed-of fish, an unqualified monster. This was long before the days when carp, tench and anything else that would sell day tickets were stocked in every commercially-viable stillwater. I could not have been more surprised if I had hooked a tarpon. It was the first proper carp, and by far the biggest fish, I had ever seen, from the canal or anywhere else. I would guess now that it weighed between four and five pounds. It was utterly enormous.

I unhooked it, lowered it with shaking hands into the keepnet and sat down, gripping my left leg to persuade it to stop trembling.

Where the heck was Pete?

I fished on, but my concentration was gone; the roach and bream seemed too trivial to waste time on now, and it was hardly likely I would get another carp.

At last, around lunchtime, I heard a shout and looked round to see Pete coming up the towpath. But he wasn't carrying a rod and there was no basket on his back. And he had someone with him.

A girl.

She was a very pretty girl; shapely, with legs. She was wearing a black leather jacket like Pete's, and she was holding his hand. I felt an odd jolt when I saw that. I had seen girls before, but I had never spoken to one, apart from my sister, who didn't count, so I didn't know what to say; all that stuff belonged to the future. I wasn't too worried, though, because I figured they would both be mightily impressed by the carp.

I smiled smugly at my pal as he and his companion drew within range, anticipating his cry as I drew the great fish from the deep, the girl abandoned on the path, the hurried footsteps on the cinders as he rushed towards me, the fevered examination on hands and knees, the dash back for rod and tackle.

I hauled. The net felt horribly light.

That was because it was empty. It was an old, much-used net and the mesh had already been darned many times with string. There was a biggish hole in the bottom and as I drew the end of the net from the water, the last tattered roach flicked through it and was gone. I stared after it in horror.

"I caught a mirror carp" I said. "A real one, enormous. At least five pounds. Took me half an hour to land it. Where have you *been*?"

Pete didn't react at all the way I'd expected. He just smiled coyly at the girl, and the girl smiled coyly at him. "Late night, last night," he said. "You should have come bowling, like I said."

I looked down at the net again and saw a flake of something translucent; a scale, rimmed with pearly smears of slime. I picked it up and Pete took it from me and studied it. The girl backed away, staging an attack of nausea. You could see that the scale was far too big to be from anywhere but the flank of a sizeable mirror carp. There was another in the bottom of the net, along with slime of an intensity small roach and bream alone could never have produced.

For a moment, there was a look of disquiet on Pete's face. "Suppose I could come tomorrow" he said. "But I'm supposed to be working, so it might be a bit tricky." He reclaimed the girl's hand, and she nuzzled his collar. "Got to get off now anyway, helping my dad on a job."

They left me there with the ruined net and started to climb back across the footbridge, horsing about and mock-wrestling with each other on every step. I heard Pete mention my name. "Yeah" she sniggered. "I really fancy boys in sandals."

Pete and I fished together again a few more times that summer and the next, but I got more and more used to going without him, and then he was old enough to leave school and get a job in a shipping office in Manchester, whereupon he announced that he was giving up fishing altogether. I have often wondered if, in the years since, he has changed his mind.

CHAPTER 2

The pool in the wood

It was as deep as England. It held
Pike too immense to stir, so immense and old
That past nightfall I dared not cast...

From 'Pike', Ted Hughes

Like all anglers with a few decades of experience under
their belts, I can look at a stream or a pond now and
know at a glance what fish it is likely to hold, if any; not
just from the colour of the water, the insect life and the nature
of the weed growing from it, but from long experience of the
way men use water and how fisheries come into being.

It was not always thus. Once I had discovered as a small
boy that there were fish bigger than sticklebacks in the world,
I assumed that every piece of water I passed contained them,
unless they were polluted to the point of being offensive.

Every farm pond, however tiny and stagnant, was surely home to the roach, perch, tench and carp I had read so much about, and every stream, however feeble, which had at least one pool deep enough to hide the bottom must surely contain marvellous trout, dashing dace and gigantic chub. Many were the muddy little ponds where I whiled away summer hours with rod and line imagining that every surfacing midge pupa was a rising fish, and many the minnow I returned in the sure and certain knowledge that where there are minnows, there are five-pound chub.

There is nothing mythical about the cherished stereotype of the small boy with the worm, the stick and the bent pin. At the age of about six, I was exactly that boy. I stole three of my mother's dressmaking pins and bent them into the shapes of hooks, then bound them together with cotton to make a treble and attached them to a length of string, which I knotted to the end of a four-foot garden cane taken from the greenhouse. Then I procured a large worm from the garden. Fearing that piercing the worm would kill it, I simply draped it over my improvised treble hook – it kept wriggling off, of course – and started pestering Dad to take me fishing. Neither he nor anyone else in the family knew the first thing about fishing, so it was some months before I was able to work out how it was actually done, longer again before I acquired some rudimentary tackle and much longer before I started to catch fish.

At first, most of them were small, and some were tiny. At the age of eleven or so my childhood fishing friend Michael Rogers and I were badly duped by the owner of a pond out in the Cheshire plain, lying among fields which have since been swallowed up under the runways of Manchester Airport. From somewhere we learned that this pond was full of carp, no less, and could be fished in return for, I think, a shilling a day. This was exciting news indeed. The next Saturday morning we cycled out there, paid our shillings and set to. The pond was circular and bowl-shaped, like a meteorite crater that's had time to grow a few weeds, and perhaps fifteen yards across. We shinned down its sides, set up our rods at water level and cast out into the carpet of duckweed.

Almost immediately I caught a fish. It was indeed a carp; a crucian carp, fat, brassy-gold… and about two inches in length. Mike caught one, then I caught another. OK, they were small even by our standards, but everyone knows that where there are small big fish, there are bigger ones. All we had to do was fish on until we encountered one of the mummies and daddies.

Of course, we never did. By the end of the day we had in our keepnets at least fifty of those little fish, all two inches long, all identical. Yet even as Mike and I poured them back through the duckweed like a shower of new-minted pennies, we were assuring each other that we had just been unlucky – we'd get among the big ones next time.

When we described our experience a few days later to an older angler we fished with on the canal, he laughed, then snorted in disgust. "He's bloody 'ad yer, 'e as," he said. "He's just shovelled them little buggers in ter tek yer money off yer. There won't be no big 'uns. Don't waste any more bloody money on 'im." We didn't. I don't think we were angry – just bitterly disappointed that our dream had died.

The Paddly Brook mentioned in the first chapter inspired further childish imaginings. Having become expert at trapping its sticklebacks and stone loaches with a net in the stony shallows, I ventured downstream to discover that there were places where the water was so deep that I could not see the bottom. I immediately assumed that this must be the home of real fish, of the kind I had encountered so far only on page 109 of the *Observer's Book of Pond Life,* given to me by my grandfather when I was about six; I still have it. In one place I found that the brook had formed an island, and on the near side of it was a pool which looked big and deep enough to hold anything I could imagine. One summer's day I set about damming the tail of it with stones and logs to raise its height, with the idea of somehow stocking it and turning it into my own little fishery. I had reckoned without the meddling of less constructively-minded boys, who persisted in wrecking my dam almost as fast as I could build it.

Below the island the river was swelled slightly by the arrival of a tributary, and it seemed to me that the streamy glide downstream between beds of water crowfoot must surely hold dace (I had never seen a dace, of course). I remember spending a Saturday morning fishing that glide with the tiny redworms the books recommended for dace, suspended from float tackle. Every time the float reached a certain point, it would shoot under. Clearly there was indeed a shoal of dace there, but for some reason I couldn't hook them. It was not until I began learning how to do river fishing on the Dane, further out towards the south-eastern corner of Cheshire, that I realised how exactly like a bite it can look when the hook catches on the bottom in fastish water.

I was slightly older when I discovered trout, in the River Birkin, a modest little lowland river meandering between red earth banks and green dairy pasture somewhere out in the soft landscape south of Bowdon and Altrincham; it flows west into the Bollin, which eventually flows into the Mersey, which at that time was polluted beyond hope and therefore an impossible barrier to migratory fish.

I cycled out one spring day to explore the Birkin, and found that it was guarded by 'PRIVATE FISHING' signs. To me the signs might as well have read 'GOOD FISHING HERE, HELP YOURSELF' and in very small print below 'but don't let anyone see you'. It seemed the fishing was controlled by an angling club and maintained as the exclusive preserve of the fly fisherman. Up to this point it had not occurred to me that we had fly fishermen in Cheshire, any more than trout. My knowledge of fly fishing was confined to a handful of sightings of much older tweed-clad anglers standing in the rivers we drove across on our Welsh holidays. I didn't think that what they were doing could be anywhere near as good as real fishing, the kind my friends and I did on ponds and canals with floats, bait and keepnets, so I had no desire to join them even if I'd had the wherewithal. But I did want to catch a trout from the Birkin.

It was time for some planning. I worked out an approach route which would allow me to hide my bicycle in woods and sneak down to the water out of sight of any roads or farmhouses. I prepared my little spinning rod, which in two parts was not much longer than the crossbar of my bike, and dug some worms. Then early one morning, I sauntered out. I trotted a worm down pool after pool (though we wouldn't have called them 'pools' then) and every once in a while the float would stab under and I would hook a rainbow trout. I caught three, each of them about a pound in weight.

I did this a further three or four times that summer, always catching a trout or two, but then I got cocky. I took Pete, my friend from the canal, to the river on a Sunday afternoon, when it should have been obvious that there would be people about and we stood a much higher chance of being spotted. The first I knew that we had been rumbled was a roar behind me. "Get out of that river!"

We didn't argue, or try to run. At least we hadn't caught anything yet. We were marched up to the farmhouse, where we were heavily reprimanded and ordered to give our names and addresses. I gave mine honestly; I think I was simply too scared to lie, and I have never been any good at it anyway, despite being an angler. Pete had no such scruples and made a name and address up, though I'm not sure they believed him. We were told the police would be calling on our parents, then sent packing.

The police never did call of course, but nor did I ever go back to the Birkin. I fished the Bollin a few times though, near Dunham. There were no 'private fishing' notices there; I don't believe anyone was fishing, stocking or managing it at all. But it was a nice little river and I caught a few roach and perch there, as I recall, and once a half-pound brown trout, the first I had ever caught.

But at that time, still water remained the greatest draw. Out on the northern edge of the Cheshire plain, between the vale of the River Bollin and the leafy opulence of Bowdon, there once lay a great oak wood. It is not there now. Should you ever have occasion to turn east from the A556 on to the M56 for Manchester and Stockport, you might wish to look down at the featureless landscape surrounding the tarmac and reflect that once, all this was trees, concealing the hidden magic of water. As ten-year-olds, newly untied from our parental apron-strings, we thought the wood limitless. To me, it was the real-life counterpart of the Wild Wood in *The Wind in the Willows*; unbounded, unmapped, unpredictable, beyond human authority and human ken. I had no doubt that it contained many wild creatures I had not dreamed of, as well as many others I had; eagles, wildcats, purple emperors, quite possibly the odd wolf, lynx or bear.

In the heart of this wood, miles from the nearest road, lay a deep, dark, forgotten pool. I stumbled upon it one day towards the end of the summer holidays when optimistically hunting rabbits with a catapult. The wood was the only place I can remember finding rabbits in boyhood; myxamotosis had practically finished them off a few years before, leaving a relict population of solitary forest-dwellers. If you walked patiently through the great wood for long enough, there was a fair chance you would start one of these lone refugees from cover, and supposedly an infinitesimal chance you might nail it with the catty, though it never happened. I would conceal my bicycle at the edge of the wood, which was private of course, load the catapult with a pebble and wander through the glades and thickets searching for my prey, relying on my youthful sense of direction to guide me back again to my bicycle in time for tea.

I wandered deeper into the wood on each visit, until one summer's day I saw something gleaming through the trees in front of me and realised I had found water. I took a few paces forward and found myself on the shores of a great pool, fully thirty yards across, surrounded by dense birch and oak woodland and ringed by a stand of tall poplars. It was invisible on all sides until you were a few yards from the bank.

This was a huge discovery. It would not have surprised or delighted me more if I had discovered an active volcano. I know now of course that the pool must have been man-made, put there long ago to rear fish, or perhaps to act as a reservoir for a farm's water supply, but I understood none of this then. To me it must have lain there forever, created by nature and unknown to all humanity except for me, a priceless secret hunting ground for a boy dedicated from birth to water and wilderness.

I memorised the way back, told my friends what had happened, and the next day, in the heart of that great wood, we went fishing.

The pond was steep-sided and dark, with none of the weedy shallows and swampy areas a natural pond exults in and which (I know now) are so important to water plants, insects, amphibians and small fish. No matter; we knew nothing of ecology, so to us this made it look all the fishier. Where there was water there would be fish, and where there was deep water there would be big fish; it was as safe as a mathematical theorem. The longer we had to wait for a bite, the more likely that it would be from something enormous. So ponds appeared to us, when we were ten years old.

We fished, floats in a line, willing them to dip, but an hour passed, and nothing happened. The other boys, none of them committed anglers like me, began to get bored. Horseplay broke out, names were called, catapults were produced. The woodland around and behind me began to echo to the sound of their play. I wished they would leave and allow me to pursue my vigil alone.

At last my friends started to gather up their scant equipment and trickle away home, leaving me alone in the heart of the silent wood. I was rummaging in my tackle basket for some fresh nylon when I heard something that made me look up with a start. From the centre of the pond, a resounding splash.

I watched the ripples spreading out from the disturbance all the way to the banks, wondering with wild surmise what monster had just revealed its presence. The idea of huge carp jumped immediately into my mind – nothing less would do, in a pond like this. I had had no experience of carp at that time, of course, other than through my reading; the canal mirror carp was to come later.

I fished on until it was nearly dark, risking severe admonishment, to say nothing of getting lost, in the hope that I would have the chance to find out, but though I stared at my float until it was lost to sight, nothing else happened.

I was not so easily discouraged, however. As a boy I would always stay by the water, and would never give up the quest until the rod froze to my fingers or my eyes blurred with exhaustion.

I returned to the pond alone the following weekend, armed with maggots, bread, worms, even some parboiled potatoes (everyone knew back then that parboiled potatoes were *the* bait for carp, though it took me several tries, a lot of wasted potatoes and a severe run-in with my exasperated mother before I had successfully made some). I set up two rods so that I could try two baits at once – I think it was the first time I had done this. One was a proper rod, my new 12ft float rod with the spliced glass-fibre top, the other was my six-foot garden cane with Uncle Alec's old Nottingham reel lashed on with string at one end and rings made from bent paper clips taped along it. I rigged up the first rod with float tackle and maggot bait and arranged things so that the maggots were 'laying on' in perhaps six feet of water. The cane rod would not cast very far, so I rigged it up with a lobworm on a big hook, anchored by a coffin lead, stripped some line off the wooden reel and then used a Nottingham cast, which I had learned about in a little handbook my father had found in the New Dog Shop in Sale, to get the bait out a few feet from the edge. It did not seem likely that I would get anywhere near the carp that way, but it was the best I could do. A second shop-bought rod with a second fixed-spool reel was out of the question; at eleven or so, I was lucky to have the one.

It was a Sunday afternoon at the end of summer and a chill north wind was beginning to harass the tops of the poplars. The pond was covered with flotillas of crispy, sepia oak and poplar leaves, all whirligigging around at the mercy of the breeze. Below the surface lurked leaves which had fallen earlier, now soggy and clingy, and each time I drew my tackle in I had to pick it free of them.

I sat there on the bank, periodically peppering the water with maggots and bits of bread flake, and waited for something to happen, as the sun sank below the trees and the wind sighed ever colder and stronger. From time to time the hook would drag on the bottom débris and a gust of wind would blow the float low in the water, allowing me to believe for a moment that some cautious leviathan was on the brink of taking the bait. Belief is everything in fishing, especially when you're just starting out.

The float started creeping tantalisingly downward again

and I gave it all my attention, hand on the rod ready to strike, just in case. And then, out of the corner of my eye, I noticed that the tip of my cane rod was moving. It had begun to trundle crabwise across the grass towards the water, like something alive. I also saw that the line was taut and vibrating, and that where it entered the water the surface was forming shimmering circles.

I leapt up, grabbed the cane and struck.

Almost always in the past when this had happened, the fish on the other end had shot out of the water on to the bank more or less immediately. Not this time. What happened now was quite different. Something pulled back, with unbelievable power. The shock of feeling such living strength on the other end of a line, so unexpectedly, has never left me.

I pulled and scrabbled, desperate to get whatever it was out of the water and on to the bank as quickly as possible, before it had a chance to let go or break the tackle. I knew little of 'playing' fish. Whatever it was pulled mightily back, with rhythmic kicks. I had never hooked a fish larger than about half a pound up until this early point in my angling career, so this was an entirely new experience.

I kept pulling in desperation, and the line held – it was heavy nylon bought for sea fishing and it was the only line I had, apart from the fine mono that was on my fixed-spool reel. The reel, however, did not. The moment the pressure of the line bore upon it, it broke free of its string bindings and fell to the ground. In horror I tried desperately to scrabble it back on to the rod, hoping somehow to rewind the disaster, if not the reel.

And then something broke the surface; something shocking,

alien and entirely unexpected.

A pike.

This early in my fishing career I was the owner of only a tiny handful of books, but along with the two-and-sixpenny junior angling guides was a leathercloth-bound volume given to me by my Uncle Alec called *The Book of the All Round Angler,* by John Bickerdyke, first published in 1888. I had read it from cover to frayed cover repeatedly, and was now reminded of a chapter called 'A Pike In The Swim'. Thanks to Bickerdyke, I immediately knew what must have happened. This was a shocking, terrifying development; though I had had encounters with roach, perch and silver bream, I had never yet encountered a pike, dead or alive. They had remained creatures of fable. This one looked monstrous, and I was nowhere near as pleased to see it as I had imagined I would be. I wasn't sure I wanted it on the bank with me, but I wanted it to escape even less, so I threw the rod down and grabbed the thick nylon above the rod tip. When I pulled on this I met no resistance, and my float came trundling towards me across the water. The pike had bitten through the cast, of course.

The great fish remained where it was for a moment, regarding me with its ancient, reptilian eyes, and then it flicked its tail and disappeared into the depths.

It was not really a big pike, of course; six or seven pounds perhaps, though it was huge to me. It was the sheer *authority* of the thing. For all the world it looked as if before biting through my line it had quite deliberately picked up my worm and swum with it to the surface to point out that my intrusion was tiresome and inappropriate, and that if it happened again it would have to have a word with my father.

It was some time before I dared to fish for pike again.

CHAPTER 3

At sea on the meres

Ye shall dream of the jewelled fishes that live in those places...

Izaak Walton, 'The Compleat Angler'

Cheshire is justly famous for its meres, flat, fertile lakes in
a flat, fertile county. They are water-filled depressions
in the plain, created some 12,000 years ago by glacial
meltwater from the last Ice Age and a rich habitat for all manner
of aquatic wildlife including, of course, coarse fish.

To us as boys in the 1960s, those meres presented quite
a challenge. The turbid waters of the canals and farm ponds
within a cycle ride of home had soon become easy meat; the
fish were under our noses, and no great mastery of angling
technology was needed to reach them. The meres, on the other
hand, were not only vast but disconcertingly clear and shallow.

I remember the afternoon Dad first took us to Pickmere

(which is named, of course, after its pike, though I don't think I noticed that back then). We waded out to the tops of our wellingtons and cast as far as we could with our cane rods and centre-pins, to find, once the splash had subsided, that our baits were plainly visible to us on the featureless muddy bottom a few yards out. Fortunately Pickmere, alone among the meres, had been pleasantly commercialised, with a funfair and a boat jetty, a miniature copy of the Windermere experience a hundred miles or so to the north. So we abandoned the muddy shore and fished from the jetty while Dad took my brother and sister round the funfair. The water here was satisfactorily deep and dirty, and as the perch that lived around it proved obliging on this and on many later occasions, I grew very fond of that jetty.

The other meres presented a much more formidable challenge. Wooded Rostherne, bequeathed to the nation by Lord Egerton as a nature reserve; Tabley, private, exclusive and paved with big tench and lost golf balls; Budworth, capable of producing hauls of huge bream, but only to serious, grown-up anglers equipped with the hardware to reach them and the time and resources for a military-scale campaign.

Yet not all the meres were inland seas. On Sunday drives out to Knutsford we would pass one that looked particularly enticing. The lake was in a place called Mere, so we decided it must be called Mere Mere, a nice bit of circular logic if you like. Curiously enough, that turned out to be exactly what it was called.

Dad let us stop to take a look, but we had to agree that it looked a bit private for fishing; big stockbrokers' houses surrounded most of it, their expensively-tailored gardens running all the way down to the placid water. There was a man there mowing his lawn who straightened up, elbows akimbo when he saw us, clearly ready to raise the voice of well-heeled authority should we dare to venture over the roadside and on to the bank. I'll take you to the canal, said Dad; this is not for us.

So a few days later, we came back on our bikes to fish Mere Mere without him. Not fair to drag him into it, really.

We hid our bikes under the trees and, taking advantage of the cover offered by the low-slung boughs of the oak and beech trees, we climbed down the banking and on to the side of the mere. It was a most enticing lake, a dozen acres in extent and largely covered by lily pads. We were at the outflow end and water from the lake was streaming down a steep concrete apron and into a culvert which ran under the road. The branches restricted our casting a bit, but the cover they provided made it a simple matter to stay out of sight of the houses and gardens as well as to hide us from the traffic on the road. Pete perched on the end of the apron and I climbed on to the base of a big tree which overhung the water. We threw in some maggots, and immediately hit paydirt. Soon we were swinging in small fish; rudd, roach and perch.

And then a curious and thrilling thing happened. I was drawing in my sixth or seventh small fish when the water swirled hugely a few yards out and something grabbed it. It hung on only for a second, but by the time I wound the rudd in it was lifeless, and bore a great puncture mark upon its flank.

Another pike! And this one did not look quite so terrifyingly large as my nemesis of the secret pond. This one I felt I had a chance of conquering in a fair fight.

Pete had wandered off along the bank somewhere, so I left him out of it – I didn't want to lose a moment. I found a big hook in my basket – I don't remember if it was a single or a treble – put on a big cork-bodied sea-fishing float and suspended the dead rudd beneath it.

The pike, or a close relative, took the rudd immediately. For a few seconds huge violence was done to my tackle, there was a slashing and a plunging and a flashing of green and white between the lily pads, and then I managed to scoop out the fish and there it was on the bank, the best part of two feet of purpose-built piscine destroyer. It certainly wasn't as big as the one that had mesmerised me in the woodland pond, but it must have weighed a good three pounds or so.

Gorgeous as the pike was, I killed it with a stick; this was before the days when it became normal to return pike, and the idea of putting such a prize back did not enter my head. Back home, my mother was impressed when I laid it out in the kitchen. It was the first one she'd seen, too. I don't think I told Dad where I had caught it. I filleted it and Mum and I cooked it together, but the flesh was the colour of old men's teeth, and the taste muddy and disappointing. Later I found that pike meat needs special treatment in the kitchen; it's better marinated, flaked and baked with potato in a pie, and better still if it comes from fresh running water.

Quite suddenly, Mere Mere was the only place I wanted to fish. We were ready to spend the rest of the summer there, heedless of the distance and the inconvenience.

But of course, it was not as easy as that. On our third or fourth visit we were caught red-handed by a man in a tweed suit who appeared from nowhere on an old-fashioned pushbike with Sturmey-Archer gears just as we had finished putting up our tackle.

"You, scarper, NOW, you little buggers," he said. "Find somewhere else to fish. If I ever catch you 'ere again I'll 'ave your rods." Pete opened his mouth to say something. "And if you give me any cheek," said the man, "the police will be here before you can take that rod down. And your parents will know all about it."

Now most boys would have taken that as the cue to, well, scarper and find somewhere else to fish. But as we packed up with him glowering over us, I felt a growing sense of resentment and injustice. I didn't like the man's aggression and what seemed a disproportionate response to a modest enough infraction. We were not, after all, trespassing on fenced-off private land or stealing sport from a water that had been prepared and stocked by others. From the overgrown character of the banks and the untrodden muddy shores it was clear that this lake was not being fished by anyone apart from us.

The man waited until he could see that the packing-up operation was past the point of no return, then got back on his bike and pedalled off towards Knutsford. I think we may have offered up a V-sign or two to his disappearing back.

I looked back at the lake lying before us, still shimmering promisingly in the morning sun. The thought of cycling the ten miles back home after such a short expedition was more than I could countenance. So I told Pete to wait, and did something I had never done before in my life. I went to see if I could get permission to fish.

I skirted the shore of the lake, dodging horse chestnut branches, to the point where a fence came down to the water, the boundary we had recognised to our little fishing zone. I wriggled round the fence, then marched up through the long grass and between the apple trees to a big white-painted detached house which I had spotted through the foliage. I found the back door, and knocked, astonished at my own bravery; a bravery born of anger and self-righteousness.

A thin, elegant woman with long white hair appeared; she looked surprised, even alarmed, but not annoyed or angry.

"I'm very sorry to bother you, but I wonder if it would be all right to fish in the lake from the end of your garden?" I said.

She looked me up and down. "Oh yes, I suppose so" she said. "I thought you were one of those awful gipsy boys. You can fish there if you like. But it is terribly muddy, I do hope you'll be safe."

I assured her that we were anglers of great experience, and certainly more than a match for a little mud. She gave me her blessing and disappeared back inside, and I charged back off down the garden again to fetch Pete. I had learned a new trick, one that still comes in handy occasionally.

We fished for most of the day from that garden, but we caught, as I remember, little or nothing. The lake was hopelessly shallow here and if you tried to cast to what looked like deeper water you simply got your tackle snagged on the lilies, or lost it on the branches overhead. I didn't think the woman's indulgence would stretch to letting us cut branches off trees or pull out lilies even if we had the means to do so, and fear of the man on the bike ruled out a return to the byewash, so we didn't bother with Mere Mere any more after that.

I think it must have been the following season that Tatton Mere opened for fishing for the first time. Tatton is a particularly handsome expanse of water set amid rolling green parkland, a joint effort by the aforementioned ice age, which put the valley there, and the guiding hand of 18th century man, which, through a little strategic landscaping, made rather more of it. The estate owners had stocked it handsomely with roach, bream and perch and announced its opening in the local press. The fishing area was to be confined to a few hundred yards of the west bank, permits would cost ten shillings, and fishing would begin, as I recall, at 9 am and finish at 9 pm.

Now back in 1962, ten shillings was two weeks' pocket money, and a heck of a lot to ask for a day ticket for coarse fishing. I could have a day at King George's Pool or on the River Dane for a tenth of the price; most of the waters I fished cost nothing at all. Pete and I discussed the problem, and it didn't take long to come up with the solution – we would just have to go poaching again, and serve them right.

That Sunday, posing as the innocent offspring of day trippers, of which Tatton had many, Pete and I cased the mere and its approaches covertly through my father's binoculars. Soon we had it all worked out. We would strike from the east bank at dawn, long before the official start time, camouflaging our cycles under bracken and approaching the secluded shore from the cover of the woodland. We would fish from concealed positions behind the curtain of reeds that fringed the shore. As soon as the legitimate anglers started to appear on the western bank we would melt away back into the woods and be away on our bikes before the fish, and their owners, knew what had hit them. If it all went according to plan, we would do it all over again, just as often as we liked.

Unfortunately my sense of righteousness over the ten-shilling tickets made me indiscreet and my parents got wind of the plan before it left the drawing board. Wearily, my father agreed to buy me a day ticket, on condition that this would be strictly a one-off. Next time I would have to pay for it myself, even if it meant funding it with a paper round.

I don't remember if my big day at Tatton was opening day itself, but it must have been soon after – the banks were lush and green and as yet uneroded by boots and baskets. The water was disconcertingly clear, and you could see the bottom sloping away towards the unfathomed depths of the lake. Fifty pegs had been placed in the ground at intervals of a dozen yards and mine, I think, was number 16.

A whistle was blown to signal the off, and the other anglers, all of whom were grown-ups, sent their floats and leger rigs whizzing off to the horizon. Try as I might, with my hybrid cane and glass-fibre rod and bottom-of-the-range Intrepid Standard fixed-spool reel, I could not compete. I spent half an hour or so manfully trying to get my porcupine quill float out into a useful depth of water before the man on my left, a youngish chap who was legering with a hinged bite indicator clipped under the butt of his rod, came to my aid and rigged me up with a sliding float – a foot of peacock quill, painted with black and white bands like a zebra crossing, with an orange tip. Fifty-odd years on, I still have it. He showed me how to tie a piece of rubber band to the line to stop the float at the appropriate depth, and I threaded on a sliding lead and mounted a bunch of maggots on a size 12 hook to nylon. Then I cast the rig out and watched it proudly riding the waves, way out in big fish country at last. Never have I felt a greater sense of anticipation.

After a while the man's bite indicator lifted and he struck and the rod bent round. He pumped and pulled and within a minute or two he had landed the most spectacular perch I had ever seen. It must have been closer to two pounds than one, and glowed like something from a coral reef, far more brilliant than the perch of my dirty old canal. This would of course have been because of the clear water it was living in, a point I did not appreciate at the time.

He put it in his keepnet and cast back again. Our baits were only a few feet apart, so by now I was watching my float so hard my head was swimming.

There was an oldish chap fishing a few pegs away to my right and I had noticed that he was throwing groundbait in, sticky balls of dough and maggots, slinging them way out into the lake and then casting a leger after them. After a time I realised that a crowd had gathered round his peg and then saw that his rod was hooped over. I ran along the bank to join the spectators. In the fish came, kicking and flapping, and I saw that it was a bream, a huge one, as big as his landing net. It was the biggest fish, and the first common bream, I had ever seen. By the end of the day the man had caught six bream, all as big or bigger than the first. All weighed over six pounds and the biggest went nine and a half, which would then have been only four pounds short of the British record. The catch, complete with photo, was the lead story on the front page of the following week's *Angling Times*.

Meanwhile back at peg 16, my float rode on undisturbed. Dad brought me something for lunch, then wandered off to look at the Hall and its collection of paintings and statuary. Again. I did not have the biggest or the wealthiest dad among my buddies, but I surely had the kindest and most patient.

And then my Belisha beacon of a quill heeled up in the water and dipped down and I struck, and suddenly it was all happening to me.

I pumped and wound against a heavy, kicking weight, scarcely able to believe I had hooked a fish of my own at last. I could not wait to see what it was – a whacking great perch, like my neighbour's? Or perhaps it was one of those monster bream?

It was neither. It was a roach, the most beautiful, perfect roach I had ever seen, and it weighed one pound six ounces, putting it clearly ahead of my previous best – and I had caught a lot of roach, even then.

I was beside myself with pride and delight. I put the roach into my keepnet and cast back in, full of confidence now, and a few minutes later much the same thing happened again and out came another roach, a twin of the first. A photographer from the *Sale and Stretford Guardian* was on hand and he got me to pose with the roach. The picture appeared in the following week's paper; not quite as good as *Angling Times*, but it would do for me.

My friend had caught nothing more since his big perch and I remember wanting to try to help him level the score. But he did not seem as interested in receiving advice as in giving it, and he just fished on. I don't think he caught anything else.

Later that season I fished at Tatton again, at my own expense this time. I was feverish with anticipation and quite unable to sleep the night before, but of course the fishing was nowhere near as easy; fish don't take long to learn about hooks and baits. The bream maestro was there again, but I don't think he caught anything at all. Nor did I.

I have wandered back to Tatton a few times over the years, with girlfriends or wives on Sunday walks, or with my children.

Nearly half a century on, anglers still fish along that carefully pegged-out stretch of the west bank, and sometimes they catch big fish; in 2007 I read that someone had landed a 46lb carp. But those early experiences on the meres taught me of the value of getting away from the crowd. These days, I would rather fish unknown water from untrodden banks, and take my chance on what I catch.

When I moved south to Bristol in the early 1970s I found a feast of good coarse fishing on the Bristol Avon, the River Chew and in various ponds and lakes around Somerset. I was well aware of the great reservoirs of Chew Valley Lake and neighbouring Blagdon, but these were the preserve of fly-fishing for trout, a sport which still didn't appeal; I couldn't see the point of dragging artificial flies around or of knowing that you were only going to catch one kind of fish. However Bristol Water had another reservoir at Cheddar and this one was reserved for coarse fishing, so I drove out to take a look.

Cheddar is the archetypal concrete bowl reservoir, contained within a circular bank of stepped concrete. That doesn't sound too attractive, but when I got there I stepped over the parapet to find that the reality was much more interesting. For a start, the water was so clear that I could see down to the bottom in something like ten feet of water. A healthy growth of weed was producing an alluring ozoney smell, which, together with the clarity of the water and the wave action being generated by a fresh westerly, gave me the pleasant sensation that I was at the seaside. This was very different from the flat, muddy meres of Cheshire.

I tackled up with the same deep-water sliding float rig I had used at Tatton, and before long I started catching perch –

big ones. As I recall the average was about 12 oz to 1lb, with some bigger fish up to a pound and a half. Thanks to the clear water they were far more brilliantly coloured than any perch I had seen before, apart from the Tatton fish that is, and a net of a dozen or so of them made a very impressive sight.

Soon after this my long-time angling buddy Dave Burr joined me for an outing, and we caught more beautiful perch. My biggest was 1lb 14oz. One day I brought a girlfriend along, made up a rod for her, put on a worm and showed her how to cast. She immediately caught a perch weighing 2lb 2oz, which forty-odd years on is still bigger than any perch I have ever caught deliberately, though I have taken several over two and a half pounds on the fly at Chew, where perch are numerous and of course regarded as a nuisance. I must say that having longed as a boy to catch big perch, I have since found that they are a species that lose their looks as they get bigger, to the extent of making you realise where the term 'coarse fishing' came from. I feel the same about chub, having caught five-pounders from the Wye.

We also tackled up for pike, and we caught those too. They were as richly coloured as the perch and as sizeable. I think the biggest I took was 14lb, but Dave had a bigger one (as usual). Pike look just great in large sizes.

There were roach too at Cheddar, specimen roach, but they were so elusive that we never did catch one, though I briefly got into a shoal once and hooked one that would surely have broken the 2lb barrier; sadly it slipped the hook as I reached for the landing net.

And then there were the eels. I don't remember how we

knew about them – perhaps someone tipped us off, or did we spot them in the clear water? We caught quite a few of them with legered lobworms, and compared to the eels we had caught before in ponds and streams, they were gigantic. Big eels don't cover you with slime and tie your tackle in knots as smaller ones do – they are much more likely to simply break it. It was Cheddar that gave me the biggest eel I have ever caught, at close to 4lb.

In the summer of 1978 I paid a solo visit to Cheddar and was dangling a worm for the perch in bright sunshine when a fish cruised past of a kind I had never seen in the reservoir before; a rainbow trout. I had caught quite a few rainbows by now, but nothing remotely as big as this one; it looked huge. Feverishly I wound in, pulled the float down until it was a foot above the hook and cast out in the direction in which the trout had gone. It took the worm immediately and shot off for the horizon, porpoising out of the water two or three times. The bale arm on my fixed-spool reel spun furiously, but somehow everything held and I calmed the fish down and coaxed it into the net. The trout weighed 3lb 10oz. My left leg trembled for some time. This was by far the biggest trout I had ever seen on the bank at that time, let alone caught myself.

Not long after this, the bailiff appeared. He told me Bristol Water had released a few rainbows into the reservoir to see how they got on; this was the first time anyone had caught one of them, as far as he knew. He told me something of the fishing on Chew and Blagdon, about the dashing rainbows and the big browns, the great fish that could strip your reel down to the backing. I was thrilled by the capture of that unlucky rainbow, but I realised it had been a freak event, and if I was to have any chance of repeating that dazzling experience there was nothing for it to abandon my absurd boyhood principles, overcome my prejudices and finally join the fly-fishing brigade.

CHAPTER 4

Shark & baked beans

Oh the fishes will laugh as they swim out of the path
And the seagulls they'll be a-smilin'

Bob Dylan, 'When The Ship Comes In'

The warmth and hospitality of the people, the timeless grandeur of the scenery, the fascinating cultural heritage – all these are excellent reasons for taking a short spring holiday in West Wales. They are not the reasons I went there, however, on a wet Sunday in May in 1972; I went because of a girl. Perhaps it would have worked better if I could have persuaded her to come with me.

She had been playing hard to get, and making a touchingly convincing job of it; moving to another town, changing her job and refusing to return my phone calls – the things women will do to keep a chap guessing. When she finally revealed during a particularly monosyllabic discussion over the phone that she was planning to get engaged to Neil from the *Leicester Mercury* I realised that a dramatic gesture was called for to save the situation, and hitting the road to some distant shore without leaving a forwarding address seemed just the ticket.

I had just splashed out on a 1966 tartan red MGB roadster with the original wire wheels, which made her behaviour seem even more perverse. Into it I packed a blue Pioneer one-man tent borrowed from my friend Adrian, a portable gas stove, some cans of baked beans, bread, biscuits and ginger beer and my sea-fishing tackle, and into the seat which only 36 hours previously had supported Jenny's shapely form I strapped my guitar. It wasn't much of a substitute, but it seemed to go with the part.

"All my bags are packed, I'm ready to go," I said to my parents. They nodded understandingly. "I'm heading down a long, lonesome road. I can't help but wonder where I'm bound. Oh, and if Jenny phones, could you leave a message at the Green Dragon in Pembroke."

I drove across Cheshire and down through the length of Wales on a day as drab as tapioca pudding and arrived in Pembrokeshire to find that almost everything was closed. I had been imagining a nice little campsite, not too crowded, where I could pitch my tent for ten bob or so, quietly slip out the guitar and draw a small but sympathetic crowd, but I couldn't find one, so I drove on and on around endless dripping, bracken-draped lanes looking for a bit of ground that didn't have crops or cattle on it. In the end, as dusk was gathering, I pitched the Pioneer in a deserted car park which served a place called Barafundle Bay.

I was happy enough with this as a starting point for my voyage of self-discovery because I could get some fishing in before taking on the full responsibilities of a relationship with Jenny. The angling section of *Holiday Wales!*, the little booklet I had bought on the way, mentioned nearby Stackpole Head as a good 'Angling Station' and advised: 'Much good sport may be enjoyed by the Angler who is willing to brave the steep Cliffs and occasional Severe Weather Conditions along this part of the Coast. Caution: Never attempt to Climb Cliffs Alone and do not venture out without Consulting Tide Table and Advising Coastguard. Bass, Wrasse, Pollock (sic), Dogfish, Bull Huss'.

I had been hoping to try a cast or two before dark, but there was no time to collect any bait and it was such a miserable evening that it was pretty much dark already, so I just heated a can of baked beans on the Primus and sat there listening to the drizzle on the tent.

Up to now I had been delighted by the Pioneer, which, from the outside, was small and compact and hence very easy to carry and erect. From the inside, it was less convenient. If I stretched one way I hit my head on the pole, and if I stretched the other I could feel wet grass on my feet. Sitting up was out of the question. I wriggled into my sleeping bag somehow, using my car rug as extra padding, and tried to read more of *Holiday Wales!* but my torch gave out, so I had a nice early night; about half past eight, I think. Some time in the night I woke, thinking Jenny was there in the tent with me, and realised after a few seconds of disorientation that this must be because I could still smell her Sea Jade on the car rug.

I was up and out of my sleeping bag soon after dawn, heating up some more beans and swigging a bottle of ginger beer, and wearing all three of the sweaters I had brought to try to get warm. I was in no hurry to face the exposed south flank of Stackpole Head, but there was absolutely nothing else to do but go fishing. So by the time it was fully light I had zipped up the tent, leaving my possessions jutting out all over like the extremities of a badly-wrapped Christmas present, and was up and away with rod and bait bucket.

No sun was detectable, but at least the drizzle had dried up. I plodded up the path to the cliff edge and looked over. The coast of the Castlemartin Peninsula stretched away from me, rocky, rugged and deserted. It was very nice, though not, if you get my meaning, terribly convivial. The sea was empty of ships and the only clue that I had not been whisked back to a time before mankind walked the earth was a line of lobster-pot floats. Certainly there were no actual humans, which was as expected, although just one would have been nice; preferably the one with long dark hair fastened in an alice band and wearing a kingfisher-blue jersey mini-dress.

I followed the cliff path down to a little inlet where I could see a patch of kelpy sand and spent an hour or so turning over boulders and delving in rock pools for bait. I found several crabs, though none of them were at the soft or peeler stage, and some small rock fish, including what I later learned was a Cornish sucker, a peculiar flattened creation with a red and blue eye pattern on its back and a huge sucker on its belly. I also managed to catch a couple of white ragworm, that rather unpleasant, fringe-footed annelid which looks like an ordinary ragworm that has been put through a sandwich toaster on the lowest setting. All in all I felt this collection gave me a fair chance with the Bass, Wrasse, Pollock, Dogfish and Bull Huss.

I walked on along the headland, thinking that the deeper the water, the better the chance. I did not know much about bass then.

The top of Stackpole Head was flat and wet and, to my astonishment, absolutely hopping with rabbits. I found a sharp pinnacle of rock which stood slightly out from the main land mass and appeared to offer a good vantage point. It took me quite a while to reach the pinnacle, which proved a little on the steep and treacherous side, even for a pinnacle, and although I was now wearing only two sweaters I was extremely warm when I finally got there, and had to take them both off.

The water below me was most impressive – clear, green and very deep. I had done some of this kind of fishing on family holidays in Cornwall and once plumbed the depth off Cudden Point, near Marazion, at thirty feet at high tide; I thought this looked deeper.

I despatched a blenny, attached it to a biggish hook on a paternoster rig and lobbed it out a few yards. It hit the water with a satisfying splash and line poured off the fixed-spool reel until the lead hit bottom. Easily thirty feet, I thought.

Nothing happened after that for a very long time, apart from me putting the sweaters back on. The sea just kept rolling past, grey-green and morose, with gulls flicking and wheeling above it, and slowly the tide got under way and the waves began to lick the base of my pinnacle.

By midday I had finished the ginger beer and the chocolate digestive biscuits I had brought with me and begun to wish I had another packet, but not as much as I wished that Stackpole Head had a fish and chip shop. I could, of course, pack up, walk back to the car and go and look for one, but that would leave me with nothing to do for the rest of the day, unless I wanted to walk all the way back again.

Then the rain stopped at last, a rag of fresh blue sky appeared and a patch of welcome sunlight raced towards me across the surface of the sea. I looked down into the water, now illuminated rather beautifully by the sun, and saw a shoal of brit swim past, followed by a small group of undersized mackerel and two sharks.

Sharks?

I glimpsed them only for a second, brownish, long and pointed. I thought perhaps it had been a trick of the light, or too much ginger beer, but a few moments later they came back – they were obviously patrolling a circuit – and I was able to check.

They were unquestionably sharks, and they looked all of six feet long. Not big by global shark standards perhaps, nothing to close a resort for, but vastly bigger than anything I had seen in water before, apart from seals.

That afternoon in Pembroke I bought a sea angling book and looked them up. Blue shark? Wrong colour. Porbeagle? Wrong shape. Great White? Wrong size. They were tope, of course. Junior sharks, but sharks nevertheless.

Wales Angling Guide by Clive Gammon actually mentioned Stackpole Head. I have it still. 'Rock fishing for tope is excellent from June to October' it says. 'Fish up to 60lb are encountered. They come in any time but are most likely around high water'.

To catch a shark – now that would be something. I thought the fish I had seen looked to be all of 60lb. I imagined the long wait, the twitch at last on the rod tip, the line pouring off the reel, the strike, the awesome power of the biggest creature you are likely to catch on rod and line from British soil. I thought of the triumphant arrival at the *Angling Times* report station, the cheering onlookers, the eager photographers and reporters, the heroic homecoming. An MGB with wire wheels *and* a six-foot shark – surely enough to melt any girl's heart.

So I bought a parcel of mackerel, some 30lb line and a packet of big hooks and spent part of the evening tying up a couple of traces with some wire I had for pike.

Tuesday dawned warm and dry and I yomped back to my pinnacle to do battle. I attached one of the mackerel and hurled it out as far as I could into the sea. My rod was the heaviest one I had, a ten-foot glass fibre spinning rod with an unusually fast taper, but it was not really heavy enough – about 2lb test curve, I imagine – and the new line didn't flow very well off my fixed-spool reel. I didn't dare lean too hard into the cast in case the tip broke, so I cast carefully, with an exaggerated sweep. Try as I might I couldn't get the mackerel much more than twenty yards out, but the tope had been under my feet, so that ought to be enough.

It was a much sunnier day and there was plenty going on down in the green depths beneath my perch. The water teemed with brit, again punctuated by small groups of mackerel and what I thought were bass, though they might have been mullet. I also saw a garfish and what can only have been a small ray of some kind.

It wasn't long before the tope reappeared. I could see them very clearly this time in the sunlit water. They looked dapper and purposeful, like mafiosi on their way to see to someone who had broken the code of silence, and though their tails hardly seemed to flicker they were past me in no time. Perhaps they weren't quite six feet long, but they were certainly very large.

I leaned back to enjoy a bit of sunshine, and realised I could hear a faint, subterranean throbbing sound; most odd. The throbbing changed to a whine and from round the cliff to my right there came a canary-yellow helicopter. It kept on coming until it was opposite me, then throttled back. The pilot did a handbrake turn and the helicopter skidded to a halt about fifty feet above the sea, directly over the spot where my bait was lying. The waves flattened impressively.

Was I poaching, and they'd called in the water authority flying squad? Was this an MoD range, and me in the way of someone's artillery? Or perhaps lobsters were making people's fortunes around here and this was simply one of the fishermen come to check his pots. I was baffled, and slightly annoyed at the disturbance to my sport.

The door of the helicopter opened and a man with a megaphone appeared.

"A wwww mmmm ba ba ba" he said through the megaphone.

"Morning!" I called back.

"A www mmmm BA BA BA BA."

"Nothing yet. Fishing for tope, you know."

"A www mmmm ba ba ba WAA WAA WAA!"

The man pointed at me, then at the cliff above, then at me again, then to the interior of the helicopter, and then went back to the beginning and did it all again. He looked like a guide explaining the Tower of London to a party of unusually stupid tourists.

It dawned on me that perhaps he was worried about my

safety.

"I'm OK" I shouted into the breeze. "Fine. No problem." I displayed a cocked thumb; two cocked thumbs. Then I made rock-climbing motions with my hands, and gave him the thumbs again, complete with a jaunty smile to demonstrate how very much at home I was on my pinnacle. I hoped he wouldn't try to land – there really wasn't room for all of us.

The man gave a dismissive wave and slammed the door of the helicopter. The pilot released the handbrake and they did a wheely, or whatever the aeronautical equivalent of a wheely is, and shot back the way they had come at forty-five degrees to the vertical.

Of course – not only had I Climbed Cliffs Alone, I had done so without Advising Coastguard. I had probably already cost the rescue service several thousand pounds. I felt dreadfully guilty, but there didn't seem to be much I could do about it, other than to put my loose change into the next RNLI box I saw.

Not long after that, with the tide approaching full, something plucked at the rod top.

I drew some line off the reel so that whatever it was wouldn't feel any resistance and held a loop of nylon loosely between my fingers. I waited, not breathing.

The tip of the rod bobbed again and the loop was drawn from my hand. I pulled off some more. The tension was quite intolerable.

Then the line started to chatter out over the open bale arm, so I closed it, lifted the rod and struck.

I felt a stupendous weight, and pulled back as hard as I could. The thing on the other end kicked very hard a couple of times, and then everything went solid. It stayed that way, with me pulling this way and that, until at last something gave and I wound in. The top swivel was still there, but that was all.

It had never really seemed likely that I would catch a tope, and I didn't think that whatever I had just lost had been a tope anyway – possibly a conger eel – so I didn't persevere. I packed up and threaded my way back through the rocks to base camp.

Back at the car park, I had company at last. A man in a peaked cap and a clear plastic raincoat was standing in front of my tent and looking down upon it as if it had just peed on his leg. He had a notepad in his hand and I realised that he was about to give it some sort of ticket.

There was just time to change direction before he saw me. I plodded along the path and across the top of the car park as if neither he, the tent nor the red sports car parked beside it were of any concern to me whatsoever.

I could feel his eyes following me as I passed, puzzling that I didn't stop.

"Is this your tent?" he called.

"Not me, chief. There's a couple of blokes fishing back there on the rocks – probably them. Some sort of problem, is there?"

"Camping here is Not Allowed. It says on the sign."

I had noticed the sign before, but assumed it was about dogs or litter. I pretended to see the tent for the first time and shook my head disapprovingly.

"I'll tell them if I see them." The man was writing a lengthy message on his pad. I carried on walking for a minute or so, then lurked in the bracken until I heard his scooter going back up the lane.

When I crept back, I saw that a sheet from the pad had been slipped underneath one of the MG's wipers. I pulled it out. It said 'To Whom It May Concern. No Camping At Any Time. Kindly Remove Tent. Camping Facilities at Three Ships Bay On Manorbier Road, Mrs Price." I wondered if the man was Mr Price.

That night I resorted to what I should have done in the first place – calling on farmers. The very first one I asked said yes, and offered free milk into the bargain. I drove into the field he had indicated, bumped across a couple of hundred yards of rough pasture, pitched the Pioneer on a flattish spot and turned in. According to the map, I was at a place called East Moor Cliff.

I wouldn't mind a pound for every time I've come across the story about the camper who is scared half to death in the middle of the night by a mad axeman/abominable snowman/ rogue grizzly that turns out to be a cow. It happened to me that night, and it completely ruined my evening. It very nearly ruined my tent too, because I was so sure I was about to be attacked that I drew my Swiss Army knife and prepared to run the intruder through like Hamlet skewering Polonius behind the arras. At the last minute I decided to let out a warning roar first, so the cow escaped with a nasty shock and its arras intact.

The next evening a family of six in a caravan arrived and parked alongside me, so I packed up the Pioneer, motored into Pembroke and sat in the Red Lion for a couple of hours trying to look as if I had more friends than Jimmy Tarbuck and that most of them were about to burst through the door and buy me a pint. It was all right while the pub was quiet, but as it filled up with cheer and chatter and I kept having to shift my position to make room for hand-holding couples I began to realise that lone holidays are not such a great idea, even lone fishing holidays, so I knocked it all on the head and drove home through the night, running down several rabbits and, I am devastated to admit, a barn owl (they were commoner then, but it was still a lousy end to a lousy holiday, especially for the owl).

I never saw Jenny again, and I have still never caught a tope.

Adapted from an article published in Waterlog *magazine*

CHAPTER 5

BBC Bill and the Last of the Summer Wine

Blagdon? How lovely! The nature you see!
But I'm home in a temper with nothing for tea.

From 'Evening Rise', by the author

The scene of my first attempt to cast a fly onto water was nearly a thousand miles away from Somerset, on a tributary of the River Aare, near Berne in Switzerland, where I lived and worked as a journalist between 1978 and 1979. It was a freezing April day when my guide Rob Brooks, a colleague in the radio newsroom where we were both employed, drove me down to the river to show me how fly-fishing worked. The droopy little rod (it was of built cane) seemed pathetically short of erectile tissue, the line clumsy and heavy, the reel absurdly simple and low-tech. It was impossible to believe that the twist of damp hair at the end of the cast could be of any interest to a fish – until there came a tug from out in the current, and for an instant the cane became alive in my hands. I had not realised that a fly line gives much more immediate contact between angler and fish than the many yards of stretchy nylon monofilament used in coarse fishing; it's like the difference between driving a sprung-for-comfort family estate and a lowered sports car. I never saw the trout responsible, which must have been a tiny fraction of the size of my Cheddar fish, but from that moment on there was a score to settle.

I started by reading up on the subject, and became captivated by *Stillwater Fly-Fishing* by Tom Ivens, perhaps the first published authority on reservoir trouting. My blood was fired further by Bob Church's book *Reservoir Trout Fishing*. On my return to Britain I was scarcely off the ferry before I was away on a mission to Veals', the Bristol tackle dealer, credit card at the ready. The expressions on the familiar faces in the coarse fishing department turned from welcoming smiles to bafflement as I walked straight past them with a brief wave and headed upstairs to the game fishing counter, where I placed myself at the mercy of Steve Wedlake, whom I knew to be the local reservoir expert. Steve kitted me out with a Hardy Richard Walker Superlite – glass fibre, in those days – an Intrepid Rimfly reel, a net with a long spiked handle, some thigh waders and a selection of lines and flies, and the next day I went fishing, on the shores of Blagdon.

I drove down on a late April morning, bursting with ludicrous optimism, and lined my car proudly up with the others in front of that famous half-timbered fishing lodge. Each of the vantage points that define the southern shore of the lake – Cheddar Water, Pipe Bay, Green Lawn, Rainbow Point, Bell's Bush – was fenced about with anglers, all wading well out from the shore and casting effortlessly out into the deep. I watched in admiration. The rod would draw back, then the line would curl and swipe overhead a couple of times and the fly would drop thirty yards or more away. I could not see how the trick was done, or even how the laws of physics allowed it. I very soon found, of course, that for me they didn't.

Never attempt to cast a fly for the first time on a reservoir. The distances required are so great and the setting so public that you might as well try to learn to ski on the downhill course at Lillehammer during the world championships. Spend a few hours on a friendly stream first, or on a little put-and-take trout fishery, where you might hope to score an early success by taking a fish under the rod top. Better still, take lessons.

God knows, I tried. For hours, I did my best to get some of those miles of pink plastic floating fly line out to an area of Blagdon that wasn't right beside my waders. I collected many tangles, and many pitying looks. One or two of the kinder anglers stopped to offer words of advice, but I needed more than advice; I needed coaching.

Eventually I crept away in shame and drove round to the relative seclusion of Chew Magna Reservoir, a modest trout lake where my coarse-fishing club had rights, to try to work it all out in private. I was relieved to find the place deserted, until an older angler appeared, and started giving instructions, uninvited. I was indignant at first, believing I could learn to cast without help, but I was being a fool. This chap showed me the basics: imagine throwing a dart, not a javelin, and let the rod and the weight of the line do the work; cast with your forearm, not your whole upper body; keep the power stroke to a narrow zone above your head instead of swinging the rod across the sky from horizon to horizon; don't defuse the momentum of the cast by feeding line with your left hand, but learn to hold it or draw it back at the right time to accelerate the line.

Eventually I learned to get the fly out seventeen or eighteen yards, and before the day was out I had caught my first fish on the fly, a one-pound rainbow which took a white Baby Doll lure. Now, perhaps, I could fish at Blagdon without reducing my angling neighbours to helpless laughter at every cast.

That lovely lake became an obsession. As the season matured from spring to summer and the water level began to drop, I returned week after week to try to come to terms with those fish. My casting improved and I was soon double-hauling a longish line, but the bank fishing at Blagdon gets harder as the season matures and I spent long hours casting for fish which either weren't there or weren't interested. A couple of times I felt a knock and realised that my fly must have had a visit from a passing rainbow, but not once did I hook an actual trout. I began to wonder if I ever would.

The protocol of reservoir fishing turned out to be completely different from the coarse fishing I was used to; for a start, it involved surprisingly little actual fishing. In summer, the older season-ticket men all followed the same routine. They would drive down to the water some time during the afternoon and pick a spot, which was usually the same one they had been fishing the night before and the night before that – unless word had got round that the fish had begun to congregate off some other tried-and-tested vantage point, in which case they would migrate there en masse. On arrival they would park their cars on the grass and dig out their landing nets. These were nearly always the standard reservoir pattern, the mesh threaded on to a collapsible triangular frame which you screwed on to a long tubular-alloy handle terminating in a spike.

Once a man had assembled his net and pulled on his waders, he would stride out into the lake and claim the most promising spot that was still available by thrusting the net vertically into the mud and leaving it there. Each net would be placed not less (and rarely more) than fifteen yards from the next – unless its owner was joining a close friend, or fishing from a sharp promontory which offered a choice of casting directions, in which case the gap would be allowed by common consent to shrink a little. As more anglers arrived and slotted their own nets into the line, a neat barricade would build up along the shore, the meshes waving in the breeze like the flags of an occupying army. The owners of the nets, meanwhile, would retire to one of the wooden benches kindly provided by Bristol Water Company, or to the tailgates of their estate cars, and while away the hours until the evening rise by sipping coffee from Thermos flask lids and exchanging banter and stories; curiously, as it seemed to me then, about almost everything but fishing.

Sometimes a newcomer who was not familiar with the Blagdon code would wade out between two of the nets while the sun was still well above the horizon and start fishing. Although the water company rulebook stated quite clearly that staking a spot was not allowed, he would very soon be put right.

Until I learned about evening rises, I thought all this a terrible waste of good fishing time. It also seemed a tragic example of putting comradeship above sport. Surely the fish would quickly be driven out of casting range by the to-ing and fro-ing of waders and the slap-slap-slap of plastic fly lines landing on water? Rather than compete with these people, who could not, I felt, be seriously trying to catch trout, I would drive past the congregation and find a quiet spot in some disregarded bay where I could pursue less suspecting quarry. But after a couple of seasons I had to admit that there was something in the old-timers' approach. In big lakes like Blagdon rainbow trout really do seem to congregate for weeks at a time in certain areas, staying there long after any creature with half a brain would realise it was tantamount to queueing up for the freezer. And in high summer, I realised that all I was achieving by starting to fish too early was to stop the fish approaching in the first place.

My friends and I referred to the older regulars affectionately as the Last of the Summer Wine crowd, after the TV series which similarly concerned men who preferred not to take their autumn years too seriously. I got to know some of them well. There was Terry, a dairyman who lived out of a Ford Granada estate and could be seen casting from Peg's Point night after night, week after week around the season. There was Mr Davies the retired schoolteacher, who would slip out early in the morning and discreetly take a good bag before leaving the water to the rest of us. Peter, I think, was also a schoolteacher, and an equally fine angler. He astonished me one August dawn by wading out beside me on Rugmoor Point with a child's fishing net, poking around in the mud with it for a while, and finally announcing triumphantly that he had recovered the contact lens he had lost the previous evening.

There was Brendan, a big broad-shouldered fellow in a flat cap who could get his fly halfway across the lake with two false casts (I once took a picture of him doing this which was used on the cover of a magazine called *Countrysport*), and Stan Pope, 80-odd going on 50, who hardly ever deviated from his favourite team of two buzzers and a green-tag stick fly. Wilf from Bath was a kindly, witty, fellow in a flat cap who was generous with advice and spare flies and would readily move over to give you fishing space if it was in short supply. There was a young chap in a Renault Fuego who seemed to know techniques the rest of us didn't, appeared always to be on the move and caught far more than his share of fish; he was Chris Ogborne, who went on to write a book about Blagdon and to become a professional guide and consultant.

My favourite of the regulars was Trowbridge Bill, who was known by some as BBC Bill because of his loud and continuous broadcasting on the subject of fish and fishing and what was wrong with the lake and his fellow anglers. Never have I known an angler put in so many hours after the trout, or enjoy the game so much. He seemed always to be there on pole position in the hotspot of the day, holding forth in his Wiltshire burr to anyone who would listen. He would chat while he was waiting to fish, while he was tackling up and while he was casting, and give us a news announcement about each missed take and a running commentary on every fish he hooked. I once took a picture of him fighting a good rainbow in the early light of a misty dawn, and that too was published, to the delight of both of us, in another country sports magazine.

But back to the fishing. It was not until the second Saturday in September of that first season that I managed to break my Blagdon duck. The day started out with a double disaster. I rose well before dawn, feeling slightly queasy after a dodgy take-away the previous night, and reached the lake at around seven to find I had forgotten my landing net. There seemed no possibility of fishing without it (these days I would shrug it off and manage somehow), and by now I felt quite ill, so I drove home and went back to bed.

I'd bought my ticket though, so there was no question of giving up. By 10 am I was back on the bank and watching my peach-coloured Cortland weight-forward floater inching gently left to right with the prevailing easterly off Rugmoor Point. After a dozen or so casts I saw the W-shaped curl straighten out and raised the rod to find that a fat and silvery 2lb rainbow trout had taken my stick fly. Half an hour later the same thing happened again, with a slightly bigger fish. They might not have been as big as my Cheddar monster, but the sense of achievement put the experience in an entirely different league. I had finally become a qualified, blooded fly fisherman.

I fished Blagdon and Chew at every possible opportunity during the seasons that followed, and as I got better at the game I caught more trout – lots more trout. Rather too often, family matters and work were neglected. I am not proud of that period of my fishing life. Happiness in fishing is not achieved by doing it at the expense of others.

One chilly Saturday at the end of, I think, the 1984 season, I was fishing in Orchard Bay when Wilf stopped by in his estate car. He asked me how it was going and I told him it was a bit slow, so he said he was going to fish further up the North Shore. A couple of hours later I heard a vehicle bumping along the track, going in the same direction, and turned round to see that it was a gleaming black hearse; it had come for Wilf, who, I learned later, had collapsed and died on the bank. Bless him – I hope he got a fish.

Although my fishing time is now spent mainly on the wild rivers of the north and west, I still go back to Blagdon and neighbouring Chew every couple of seasons or so for a few casts into the waters of memory. On a fine summer's evening with the trout beginning to move offshore, the water birds fussing over their domestic arrangements and the first buzzers or sedges coming off, I don't think there is any water where I feel more at peace.

CHAPTER 6

"You can't catch them on a line"

He who would seek her in clear streams
Let him go softly, as in a dream

From 'The Names of the Sea Trout', Tom Rawling

W hen I was a reporter on the *Sutton Coldfield News* in the 1970s I interviewed a man whose hobby was comet hunting. He had constructed an enormous telescope in a tailor-made shed in his back garden and could be found on any clear night gazing through it, muffled against the chill like an octogenarian on the deck of a liner, Phillips' Star Atlas at one elbow, mug of cocoa at the other. I suggested that after thirty years or so of this he must have chalked up quite a few comets, perhaps even the odd supernova, but it was not so. He had never spotted a single heavenly apparition that someone else hadn't got to first. I felt at the time that though this was a peaceful way to spend one's retirement, it nevertheless amounted to failure on a tragic scale.

That was before I took up sea-trout fishing.

The sea trout started it, one holiday morning in North Wales in the early sixties. As always I had to fish, so my parents deposited me on the salt marshes outside Pwllheli while they went shopping. There was no argument about it; they had learned to live with my obsession. Come to think of it, I don't remember anything being said about watching for the incoming tide, and there seemed a faint air of disappointment about my father later on when he saw me plodding safe and sound back to the car.

The watercourse which had captured my attention was a stream which flowed under the bridge at the entrance to the town and then wandered across the marsh, dividing into a series of tidal creeks. I waved my transport away and marched up to the main creek, hoping for the chance of an eel or a flounder on the making tide.

But the stream was no more than two yards wide, and worse – it was crystal clear. We didn't have any of that sort of nonsense back home in north Cheshire; our canals and rivers were good and dirty, the kinds of places a fish could feel safe in. Here you could see the bottom. Hopeless.

Although it *was* quite deep – a couple of feet, even three. I stepped carefully along the bank through the marsh grass, looking for some sign of worthwhile quarry. It would be a little embarrassing, after all the fuss, if I had committed myself to a morning fishing a water that contained nothing bigger than the odd baby flounder.

What I saw next was so unexpected, and so astonishing, that I froze in shock. Cruising up the little channel towards me in tight formation were five of the biggest fish I had ever seen. They were sleek, grey, shovel-tailed, spotted. They could not be salmon – I had never seen a live salmon, but understood they were found only in rocky rivers, separately. Trout, then? Except that these fish were monochrome from tip to tail, no reds, browns or yellows, and they were too big by a factor of about a hundred. I really couldn't think what they were, but I knew I had to catch one of them or die in the attempt.

Gathering back my wits, I crouched down and flicked my worm out into the creek. The fish kept coming; the suspense was appalling.

They reached the worm, and swept past it as if it wasn't there.

I tried again, and again the worm was disregarded, so I gave it a little jerk, the way you do with perch. The worm bobbed up in the water and the fish turned on their tails and shot back the way they had come, all the way back up the creek towards the main stream. I scrambled after them, fearing I had lost them. But two minutes later, they were back. They couldn't get away from me or the creek; they had been imprisoned by the tide.

I cast for them again. And again. I tried tying the worms in a big bunch. I tried a spinner. I tried mackerel feathers. I tried ambushing them with the shrimping net I had brought to gather bait. If I'd had my air rifle with me, I would probably have tried to shoot them. By the time my parents returned, I don't know who was closer to a nervous breakdown, me or the fish. And still I had no idea what they were.

Back at our B&B in Llanbedrog, Mrs Evans knew. Salmon trout, she said to my father. They get some big ones in the nets. Didn't he have a net with him? You can't catch them on a line. The idea of it! Poaching he was, anyway, don't let the water board catch him. Never mind cariad, have a Welsh cake.

Back home I tried to find out something about salmon trout from my library books, with little success, except to confirm that they were more generally known as sea trout and were not found in Cheshire, other than in the Dee. There are quite a few interesting things that are not found in Cheshire, so this was no great surprise. My mother had a cookery book which mentioned sea trout, but it said they lived in the sea and weighed between twelve ounces and two pounds, so that didn't fit.

I think it was the following year when I actually did catch a salmon trout. I joined the family on a day trip to Aberdaron, and looked over the town bridge (there will be a lot of bridges in this book) to see a group of slender fish holding the current in the tail of a small pool. I knew them to be trout, because when I wriggled closer and peered into the water at close range I could clearly see their spots. Trout eat worms – I knew that too. So I fished for them with worms. They weren't interested, but as with the monsters of Pwllheli, I could not accept their refusal. I just kept drifting my worm past those fish again and again, until one of them finally lost patience with me and took it. I landed it, a perfect, silvery trout perhaps ten inches long. A few minutes later I landed another. Mrs Evans confirmed that these too were salmon trout, though admittedly they were a small fraction of the size of the monsters of the Pwllheli marsh. She was sceptical that I could have caught them by fair angling, but my father was witness to that. She cooked them for us, and they were pink and delicious. That was the first time my angling efforts had ever put proper fish on the table, and I was bursting with pride.

Back home my vision of the monsters of the Pwllheli marshes faded, and in due course I was able once again to take pleasure from the pursuit of humble roach, perch and tench; there might have been trout in my part of Cheshire then, but there were certainly no sea trout.

Yet I could not quite forget them, and one of the reasons for this was Romany. If you were born in the first half of the twentieth century you might remember Romany; he was once to wildlife broadcasting what Patrick Moore was for so long to amateur astronomy. His broadcasts on the BBC Light Programme and his books (I have several of them, given to me by my grandfather) were charming, if largely invented, rambles through a romanticised North Country landscape peopled by sagacious shepherds, honest poachers and aproned farmers' wives who would pop a blackberry plate-cake in the oven the moment they heard your boots coming up the path. Not knowing that both the books and the radio programmes were fiction, I took every word Romany said literally and imagined that everything was being broadcast live from the dales and fells as his adventures unfolded. It was my grandfather who pricked the bubble. He had heard a radio documentary which had described how the sound of the March wind howling over the fells had been manufactured by moving fans around in front of the microphone, and the sloshing of boots in the stream as Romany fished for gudgeon and minnows to use as bait had been simulated by slopping bowls around in a bath in the studio.

Romany spent a lot of time in the company of two female companions of sensitive age called Muriel and Doris. Using his gaily-painted caravan (he called it his 'vardo') as a base, he was able to introduce them to many of nature's secrets, entirely without risk of exposure in the *News of the World*; this was an innocent age. Together they would ramble across fell and down dale, marvelling at the nesting habits of the curlew or the evasive skills of the hare.

There was one episode, in *A Romany On The Trail* (1934), in which Romany left Muriel and Doris safely at home pressing flowers or whatever they did when he wasn't around and went night fishing with his friend John Rubb on the local river. For sea trout. I read the description of that outing enthralled: "Then came that slow, decisive pull at my line that I had been waiting for so long. I gave a slight flick of my wrist upwards and the next moment, before I had time to call 'got him', a fine sea trout leaped like a silver crescent right out of the water, and then went back with a fine splash. 'You're into a good 'un' called John. 'Give 'im plenty of line!'"

How wonderful it would be, I thought, just you and the dark, rushing river and that mighty silver fish leaping out there in the dark, the swish of cane and silk, the clink of boots on stones, the thrilling alarm of the reel's check. But the rivers he spoke of were far beyond the range of a Sunday drive with Dad, and I had neither the tackle, the expertise nor the licence money for such exotic quarry. It would be many years before I would have any chance of following in Romany's fictitious footsteps.

CHAPTER 7

Suits you, sir

For the apparel oft proclaims the man...

Polonius, Hamlet, Act 1 scene 3

The gods do not take from a man's life the time he spends fishing, but wives and employers are less generous. That's why, when I was in regular employment, I liked to keep my fishing trips low key. If I went fishing on a weekday I either took a day's leave at short notice or timed a visit to a client so that it would end just as the trout were beginning to stretch their fins, take a preprandial stroll around the weedbeds and debate whether to whack into the buzzers or have a night on the sedges.

So I was wrongfooted when one summer's afternoon my boss popped his head round the door and said: "You go fishing at Chew Valley Lake, don't you?"

"Ah yes, Chew," I said, pretending to cast my mind back across the years to the days when I might have had leisure for such idle stuff as fishing, but actually only having to coax it as far as the previous Tuesday, when I had taken a brace of fat dawn rainbows on a buzzer from Nunnery Point before sidling into the office in time for morning coffee. "Don't have much time for that sort of thing these days, Philip," I sighed, gesturing with cheerful regret towards the pile of paperwork that lay before me.

"Ah. Shame. Well, you know Whitbread are sponsoring one of these youth sports days there tomorrow? I've already told them we've got an angler on the team here and the promotions woman is expecting you at nine-thirty. Sorry to bugger up your day at such short notice, I know you've got a lot on your plate."

I persuaded my features to sag briefly into a mask of despair, then smiled and told him that of course, we couldn't break a promise to a major client.

The brewery in question, which was then my PR company's major client, was sponsoring a series of days of sporting tuition for youngsters who lacked the means or the connections to arrange such a thing for themselves. And one of the sports was fly fishing. Back in the eighties, this was much more novel and enterprising than it would seem now.

They had booked a trio of boats and a brace of heavyweight instructors to supplement the Bristol Water team; one of the instructors was Charles Jardine, who has become a very well-known figure in the angling world. I can't remember who the other was. I felt pretty flattered to be on the guest list, until I discovered that it wasn't really I who had been invited; it was my tackle. With a dozen rodless beginners to look after, they needed all the spare gear they could get.

The sloping lawns which surround Woodford Lodge have seen thousands of newcomers to the sport make their first swishes and swipes with a fly rod, supported by the patient counselling of the men from the water company. The next morning I pulled up on the gravel behind the car park and ambled round to the front of the lodge to find that a casting lesson was already in full swing. In front of the lodge's picture window stood a row of serious-faced boys, all flailing limp arms half a beat behind the instructor. Lines swooshed and fizzed, cracking leaders, decapitating dandelions.

The instructor stopped behind the biggest boy, who was red in the face from the effort of mastering this unfamiliar skill, and put his hand on a beefy shoulder.

"Do you play cricket?" he asked.

"Yes sir."

"How far can you throw the ball?"

"Sixty yards, sir."

"Do you know what a cricket ball weighs?"

"Six ounces, sir."

"Do you know what that fly line weighs?"

"No sir."

"Less than an ounce. So don't you think you might be using just a little too much force?"

The boy gave an embarrassed smile and tried again, but this time he didn't try to hurl the wisp of wool on the end of his leader all the way to the Bristol Channel, and the line snaked out fifteen yards and dropped neatly on to the grass. I wished I'd had an instructor like that when I'd started.

I dug out the two spare rods I had brought and two of

the boys were detailed to put them up, with a little help from me. The rods were well-used glass-fibre Hardys and I had rather meanly matched them to floating lines a size too light as a measure of insurance against cricket-ball-hurling young athletes.

Outside the lodge, a brace of Volvo estates with big logos on their doors and roof-mounted transmitters drove up, and I remembered that we were going to be filmed for a television programme. A small, neat man with oiled hair and a sheepskin coat (this was in the days when all TV reporters wore sheepskin coats, except when it was very hot, when they swapped them for safari jackets) got out of one of the cars and started surveying the lodge, the flower displays, the parked cars and us. The irritation on his face made it clear that everything would have to be entirely rearranged before there was any possibility of getting the show on the road, or at any rate on to video.

Cameras were mounted, sound systems tested, microphones brandished. The lake and the lodge were filmed from twenty or thirty different angles. The boys were interviewed, the Bristol Water man was interviewed, the instructors were interviewed, the company spokesman was interviewed. All the crew needed now, they explained, were some shots of trout being caught. They were less than thrilled to learn that this might involve a certain amount of waiting.

The reporter and the cameraman were looking at the sky and discussing props and lighting angles. The sun came out and the reporter looked down at his sheepskin uncertainly. He tried undoing the buttons and tossing back his coat tails in a nonchalant manner, but it didn't seem to do the trick; he still looked like a stoat in a tea cosy. The cameraman shook his head sternly and the reporter pulled off the coat and laid it regretfully on a bench. In his shirtsleeves, he looked as if he had been plucked. Or rather, sheared.

Then he looked at me and saw the coat I was wearing. It was a well-used Barbour Solway waxproof, a standard fishing coat, as worn by many of the Chew and Blagdon regulars. Though not yet, at that time in the early eighties, by a couple of million people who had never got closer to a trout than the queue for the deli at Waitrose.

He looked down at his sheepskin and back at the Barbour and his expression said, I have seen the future, and it is not sheepskin. His eyes had a far-off look, like Mr Toad in *The Wind in the Willows* in the famous passage where a wayward motor car brings the hero's caravanning days to a dusty end and sweeps him on to his next passion. He didn't exactly say 'poop poop', but his eyes looked as if they were at least considering what the world might look like away from their sockets.

"I couldn't just borrow your coat for a moment?" he said, advancing towards it. It was clear from the look on his face that the idea that I might refuse simply hadn't occurred to him.

"Of course. All part of the service," I answered. After all, I was there to help the media.

He threaded his arms into the sleeves and looked proudly down at the result, a man who had at last found a garment worthy of his image. His grin faded slightly when he tried the pockets for size and discovered their contents; a gritty tub of fly floatant, a cloth used for removing fish slime from hands, a shrink-wrapped ham roll left over from my last outing. But he had some fun with my priest, waving it around like a truncheon and pretending to cosh the sound man.

I left him rehearsing his piece-to-camera and went down to watch the action. Down by the jetty there was much giving out of safety instructions amid jostled excitement before the boats cast off at last, each carrying an instructor and three young novitiates, leaving the water company men to look after those awaiting their turn on the shore.

The head ranger said I could have a cast or two from the bank if I liked, but I was conscious that I was technically on duty, even if only as chaperone to my tackle, so I lingered by the lodge, chatting to the people from the brewery and discussing the arcanery of the sport as knowledgeably as I could with the fisheries team.

After a while we saw that the boats were motoring shorewards. The cameraman shouldered his equipment and we plodded down with him to watch him film the catch.

But there wasn't one. Not a trout in sight. It happens, of course, even on Chew, and even with experts on hand. It particularly happens, I'm told, when you are trying to produce fish for the camera.

The boys stepped ashore, the new contingent took their places and the outboards fired up again. Having donated two of my rods and my coat, there didn't seem a lot more that I could contribute, so I decided to accept the invitation to do some fishing. I went back to the car and put up my remaining rod with a floater and a team of nymphs. I didn't bother with waders; I just took a net and a box of flies, strolled down to the lake shore to the right of the jetty and started flicking out a short line across the breeze.

There had been a good blow the previous day and the

water along the margins was rust-red with mud. In the middle of a sunny day, in mid-season, you don't expect to contact too many fish from the bank at Chew, so I was really just going through the motions in between watching the youngsters out on the water to see how they were getting on, and hoping my rods were still in the original number of pieces.

You know what I'm going to say next, don't you? You're absolutely right. I hadn't been fishing five minutes when the line drew out tight and I found myself attached to a good rainbow. The fish was nearer three pounds than two, bright silver and with a fine big tail. It had taken the green-tag stick fly on the point. I imagine it had been drawn inshore by the apparent security of the dirty marginal water.

I despatched the trout, crooked a finger under one of its gills and walked up the bank to show it to the lads. As I came over the skyline the TV crew, the water company men and a group of the boys were still standing around in front of the lodge. They didn't take much notice until they saw what I was holding. Then they took a lot of notice. The reporter and the cameraman charged down the bank as if they had spotted Lord Lucan. I was made to retrace my steps holding the fish aloft, then again with it spread between my hands to make it look as big as possible. They actually asked if I could put the fish back on the hook and pretend to catch it again, but there are some things down to which I will not stoop, even for a client.

Then it occurred to them that I was not, of course, the right person to have caught the fish, just as I had not been the right person to wear the jacket. The trout was confiscated and given to one of the boys, to be filmed all over again.

Eventually we heard a shout from the lake and looked up

to see the boats returning once more. Even from this range you could tell by the bustle and the waving that somebody had hit the jackpot. I think all the boats had found fish. The crew got what they wanted and I got my trout and my rods back. The reporter offered to buy my coat from me, but I told him it had been made for my great grandfather and was a family heirloom. I'm not sure whether he believed me, but he wasn't too pleased.

A few days later, I was watching TV when who should appear but my friend the reporter, breathlessly commenting on some neighbourly dispute or other.

And wearing a brand-new Barbour waxproof.

CHAPTER 8

A dream of silver

*The hunt for trout is a force which pulses in the blood, fills
the mind with nostalgic recollection and new hopes.*

Jeremy Lucas, 'Fly-Fisher' (1986)

At the end of the seventies I started to keep a fishing
and nature diary, which I still maintain today. Its
early pages remind me that my greatest desire at that
time was a season rod on Blagdon Lake and the time and
freedom to use it. In 1979, to be able to cast a team of nymphs
over Rugmoor Bay, Peg's Point or Green Lawn three or four
times a week from April through to October was my idea of
angling heaven.

I never thought it possible that this desire would fade, yet
it did. Somewhere around my eighth season of day-ticketing at

Blagdon, and my three or four hundredth two-pound rainbow trout (a clue for you there), I had to square up to the awful fact that Blagdon had changed. Not in reality of course; it was, and is, a long and shapely lake stuffed with long and shapely trout. It just didn't mean so much to me any more. The *need* had gone. It was like that stomach-churning realisation that having made all those promises to the girl in your life, the one you would have done anything for just to breathe the same air a few years back, you have begun to date her out of duty rather than desire, and that soon you are going to have to confess it.

I think it must also have been about this time that I read in *Angling Times* about a man called F W Holiday who had been catching some absurdly large sea trout from the Welsh rivers, just like those great creatures which had driven me to distraction on the Pwllheli marshes. It all added fuel to the fire. Clearly I would one day have to try to catch one of these fabulous fish. I now understood what sea trout were, but I also realised that catching them was going to be a tough challenge, not least because the best sea-trout fishing is done after dark in the rivers of the wild west of Britain, and hundred-mile-plus drives would be involved, along with sleepless nights; at the time it was all I could do to manage the 20-mile drive to Blagdon once or twice a month.

It was the summer road to Wales that turned pipe-dream into reality. Specifically, it was the A476 from Cross Hands to Llandeilo, an undulating byway that winds through green and lovely pastures to the bridges of the middle Towy, arguably the most productive water for big sea-trout in Britain. I was led there not initially by the desire to fish but by the new love in my life, who was born in Carmarthen on the very banks of the

Towy and wanted to show me the land of her fathers.

We peered from the bridges at Dryslwyn and Golden Grove, crossed the river inquisitively at Llangadog and Llandeilo, then completed the circuit by gliding back down the A40 on the west side of the valley and stopping the car in the layby at Nantgaredig, where we found ourselves on the threshold of the best of all the Towy's bridges. It is a fine old sturdy three-arch Welsh stone affair flanked by rolling wooded banks, and it looks on the one hand up into the famous Junction Beat of the Abercothi fishery and on the other downstream along a beguiling tree-lined run towards the tidal reaches and the sea, the place sea-trout come from.

On the shingle below the bridge, two men were fishing, following each other down at a carefully-maintained distance. They had long rods and little worm boxes clipped to their belts and they were casting into a marvellous deep green run under the trees on the far bank. I crossed the road and looked down into the swirling pool above the bridge and on its lip I saw a shoal of silver sewin, as the Welsh call grown sea trout, fresh up from the tide. They hung there, swerving and flashing intermittently like giant dace, with a few bigger ones, gunmetal torpedoes, lying more circumspectly behind them; they did not look much smaller than my old friends from the Pwllheli creek twenty-five years before.

That was it. I had to have those fish. Blagdon and its rainbows were forgotten; in fact my visits since that day have amounted to little more than the occasional nostalgic day trip.

Back home in England, I went to Georges' in Bristol and bought *Sea Trout Fishing, a Practical Guide*, Hugh Falkus' thick green bible of the game. I read it from cover to cover, then started it all over again. I still haven't finished it, of course;

it is not a book that can ever be finished.

The frontispiece of Hugh's book shows a group of men gathered on the lawn at Cragg Cottage. They look very like my father and his cousins in family photos of the period: the same languid RAF hairstyles and oddly-constructed knitwear. But these men were not carrying box Brownies and boaters; far better than that, they bore fishing tackle. They bristled with the stuff, in fact – cane rods, fly boxes, gleaming reels, big round nets at the ready. I wanted to be among those men. I wanted to be in Hugh's world even more, if that were possible, than I had once wanted to be in the world of Dick Walker and Fred Taylor, or that of Tom Ivens and John Goddard.

Falkus was (and remains) to sea-trout fishing what Romany was to early nature broadcasting and Patrick Moore to amateur astronomy. I was thrilled, inspired, by Hugh's cheery assurance that the sea trout *will* take the angler's lure in half-decent conditions, if you keep at it. In particular, it will take a fly dressed for trout in the depths of a summer night, when every other fish in the river is dormant. No one really knows why this happens, but it does, or at least it has (there are photos to prove it), and therefore presumably could again. Like comets and supernovae.

Sea Trout Fishing planted the seed and over the years that followed, the Towy watered it. They were years of great happiness. I was in love; I was moderately successful at work, with enough disposable income to buy tackle and licences; and I was living the best dream yet, the sea-trout dream. On an early trip to Swansea, her father ushered me off to Capstan House, home of the city's senior tackle shop. We climbed the stairs to the game fishing department and found huge circular salmon nets, studded chest waders that reached from floor to ceiling, gaffs and tailers, tweed hats, oddly-abbreviated wading vests. We saw long, whippy sea-trout rods, towering double-handed salmon rods, finely-machined four-inch fly reels; saw them, touched them, priced them.

I started to amass the kit that gives admission to the lovely world of the sea-trout and salmon angler. By the end of the eighties, I was pretty well tooled up. My desire for sea-trout and everything to do with them had become absolute, urgent, unquestioned, unclouded by any equivocation. It was clear that nothing could be more marvellous than to angle for this beautiful, powerful, silver migrant in the clear, rushing rivers of the west. I even found myself pitying those who had the misfortune actually to have been raised on the banks of those great rivers. I felt they could never value them as much as I did, brought up as I was in North Cheshire, with Petrochemicals on one side and Old Trafford on the other, a hundred miles from anything even faintly migratory.

I fished my socks off. I drove up and down between Gloucestershire and the Dyffryn Tywi on every occasion when later marriage to my Carmarthen girl and the demands of my little business would allow. I explored pretty much the whole river, along with a few of its tributaries. I slept in the car, or on the bank, or back home on the sofa in the afternoons.

Results were some time coming, thank goodness. I first learned many ways of not catching sea-trout. I didn't catch them by fishing with the fly when there were no fish and with the spinner when there was no water. I carefully avoided the productive tails and glides, concentrating instead on the deep holes where fish lie but do not take. I failed at night when the river was rising and by day in a spate so big you couldn't find the river, let alone the fish.

I did, however, learn quite a bit about my beautiful, brave, infuriating quarry, not just by studying the writings of Falkus and others (whose advice, I eventually realised, did not always fit the Welsh rivers) but sometimes by meeting people who had caught them personally, as it were. I learned about the sea trout's temperament (unpredictable), its feeding habits (it doesn't have any) and the best time to fish for them (up to around twenty years ago.)

By the start of the nineties I had widened my reading from Falkus to Harris & Morgan, Dawson, Bluett, Bingham, Bridgett and G H Nall. By diligent stalking I had discovered where my quarry liked to lie by day (deep, shaded pools protected from anglers by overhanging trees). I had found out what flies they had been taken on by those who had done it, and amassed a large collection of free samples from fellow anglers who took pity on the sheer absoluteness of my failure. I had netted, weighed and admired several sea trout for other anglers. But as far as the actual capture of the wretched creature by my own hand was concerned, I remained a sea-trout virgin, nay, a sea-trout spinster. I was a sea-trout expert who had never caught a sea trout.

By 1992, what had started as a nice idea for something to do on a summer's evening had developed into a quest on a par with the search for a proof of the Riemann Hypothesis. Giving up was out of the question. Compared to me and my attempts to catch a sea trout, the hero of *The Old Man and the Sea* was enjoying a couple of hours away from the wife and kids.

Once again most of that season passed without incident, except that I did catch a brace of fourteen-inch finnock, first-season sea trout. On lesser rivers this sort of fish would no doubt go in the record book as a sea trout, but not on the Towy.

August Bank Holiday of that year was wet. On the Friday, when I arrived, the river was big and brown and unfishable. But I am an optimist (I expect you've worked that out by now) so I was by the river at eight o' clock the next morning just the same, putting up my spinning rod.

The river had run off a little during the night and was looking rather promising. And as I strolled down the bank towards the main holding pool on our club stretch, which, aptly enough (as you will learn), is called the Crewil Pool, I saw that Gwynfor, the club secretary, was standing beside the run-in to the pool and that his rod was very, very bent. By the time I reached him he was in the act of landing a fresh-run twelve-and-a-half-pound salmon.

We gazed at the fish, big and silver and miraculous in the grass, and Gwynfor put his hand on my elbow.

"Have my spot" he said. "I'm going home now. That will do for me."

I cast, and on the very first retrieve my Irish minnow (the go-to sea-trout lure at the time, a more sophisticated version of the Devon minnow) was followed by a sea trout of between four and five pounds which turned away at my trembling feet. The same thing happened again on the second cast, with a slightly smaller fish. With the whole weekend in front of me, I dared to think the impossible; that I might get one. But no more sewin followed the Irish minnow, or the Toby I tried next, or the Mepps that followed it. Everything remained quiet for another hour or more, by which time I had reached the wooded tail of the pool. The current was very heavy here and I felt my Mepps wasn't getting deep enough, so I added a large drilled bullet and started casting upstream to give it a chance to sink.

And then – the rod curved round and I struck and felt a double kick and found that reality had been suspended. I knew that someone was playing a fish, that the fish must be a sea trout and that the person playing it must be me, but it all seemed to be happening in a parallel universe on the other side of a soundproof window.

The person I knew to be me played the fish we both knew to be a sea trout with careful desperation. The fish made some worrying charges towards the sanctuary of the rooted bank above, but I pulled it back and at last it came into view, turned on to its side and rolled towards the net. It looked to be a sewin of between five and six pounds. It looked very beautiful.

I found I couldn't quite reach the fish with the net as it was, so I allowed the line to slacken off a fraction as I extended its handle. The sewin kicked, and the Mepps flew high in the air.

The club had constructed a sort of bus shelter by the tail of the Crewil and I sat inside it for a while and got a grip. I remember a pied flycatcher looked in to see if I was all right.

After a few moments I got back to my feet, checked the hooks of the Mepps and cast out again into the same spot. I don't know whether it was the first cast or the second but I do know it happened almost immediately; again the rod hooped over and again I felt a kick, but this time it wasn't just heavy; it was elephantine.

I resisted as hard as I possibly could, and according to my diary I was using 17lb running line and a 15lb leader, so it should have made some impression. But each time I pulled, the fish just gave another huge, contemptuous kick and ripped off a bit more line. Then it started boring downriver, into the rooty fastnesses of the pool, and I pulled harder than ever, fit to break the tackle. The fish was not in the least impressed, and the reel's slipping clutch, which was wound down tight, gave with a sound like a lorry braking on concrete.

Once the fish had put fifteen yards or so between us, it got bored with the whole business and just sat down on the bottom of the river. I tried to make it change its mind by pulling this way and that, but it simply ignored me. After a while I had to let my arm rest, so I gave the fish slack, as far as it was possible to do so in such heavy water. The river was clearing, though, now, and I noticed something that I had not been able to see before, something which the regulars, I later learned, could have told me about if I'd asked.

A sunken tree, right in the middle of the river, directly between me and the fish.

I waited a long time, but eventually I just had to pull for a break. The Towy has some monster sea trout, but I am pretty sure from its laid-back attitude to the whole affair that this fish was a salmon. Since that day I have managed to grass some decent specimens of both species from the Towy, but never again have I hooked one as obdurate, as effortlessly in control, as the fish that engulfed my Mepps on that August Bank Holiday Saturday of 1992.

The river was unfishable again the next day (though I tried anyway, for a while). But on the Monday it had run off again and was looking just about perfect. The morning was uneventful, but around lunchtime one of the other anglers took a nice grilse from the Crewil and then someone else took a brace of sea trout, one after the other... my packed lunch was forgotten.

I had to leave around four o'clock, but Clive, the man who had taken the grilse, insisted that I have a cast in his spot first. Word had got round about my double tragedy, and the other anglers were keeping a respectful distance from me.

I was fishing a worm, because the colour had run off a bit and – well no one can keep casting and retrieving a spinner all day; that way lies madness, to say nothing of terminal backache. I flicked it out, weighted with a lump of Plasticine on a thin nylon 'rotten bottom', a trick I'd developed for barbel and chub.

The worm and the Plasticine trundled down the pool for a few feet and stopped. I lifted the rod to find out why and – well, must I go on? All you need to know is that it was another fresh-run sea trout, that it was at least as big as the first and that I had hooked it from a high bank between two trees on a size 8 hook at the very tip of the snout. Oh, and that I had left my net further up the pool (having trained on reservoirs, I hadn't yet learned to use a proper salmon net with a sling). A kindly fellow angler came running down with it when he heard my shout, but by the time he reached me, the fish was not there any more.

Serves me right. I should have listened to Mrs Evans. Perhaps you really couldn't catch them on a line.

CHAPTER 9

The wildest fish

The sea is the land's edge also, the granite
Into which it reaches...
The sea has many voices,
Many gods and many voices.

T S Eliot, the Dry Salvages (Four Quartets)

T he sea is the greatest hunting ground of all, and the bass is surely its finest and wildest quarry. There is nothing else around these islands to match those silvery mailed flanks, the bristling fins, the ravening gape, the predatory dash and verve.

I found out about bass by accident at the age of eleven, by catching two of them from the estuary of the Conwy in North Wales during one of several summer holidays at the home of my great aunts in Deganwy. I rigged up my boy's spinning rod with mussel bait, which was all I could find, hoping, as the brown tide barrelled past, that it might give me a flounder. Instead I dragged two beautiful bass from the torrent on successive casts, to the disbelief and disgust of the grown-up anglers either side of me. One of them, however, was kind enough to weigh them for me, at one pound twelve ounces and two pounds twelve ounces.

I marched my shining brace back up the cliff road to Alderwood, bursting with pride and fully expecting a hero's welcome. My parents were impressed, but neither they, nor Mrs Jones, the cook and housekeeper, nor my great aunts seemed to know what to do with them. "Have you had good sport?" Aunty Phee called cheerily, when she saw me arrive in the hall (she had told us that she had been taught to say this to returning anglers rather than the potentially embarrassing "Have you caught anything?") She did not even notice that I had indeed had good sport until I thrust the fish under her nose, at which point she looked rather shocked.

My mother would willingly have cooked them for us, but the kitchen was Mrs Jones's domain and Mum was not the type to flout protocol. Because I did not know enough then about the eating qualities of bass to fight their corner, my two beautiful fish ended up buried under the compost heap, an outcome for which I have never quite forgiven any of those present, including myself.

Fast forward a dozen years or so to the 1970s, a time when most of my fishing hours were spent on the shores of canals and reedy lakes. I was living in Bristol by then, and had noticed that the Dorset coast was not too far away. I acquired the habit of driving down to the sea on my day off, which was usually a Friday (as a newspaper reporter I usually opted to work Saturdays, as the hours were shorter for the same pay). There had been a number of reports in the angling press of very big bass being caught from Portland Bill, and I resolved to try for them.

On arrival, Portland Bill reminded me of Stackpole Head and the tope. The water was as precipitously deep and as wonderfully green, and when I saw the shadow of a group of mackerel go gliding past, I felt success of some kind was guaranteed. It wasn't. As I recall, I caught nothing in my several trips to Dorset but wrasse and small pollack.

The first decent bass I saw was the result of a chance encounter with a French angler one summer in a harbour in Brittany – Brest, I think. Spying him at the end of a jetty, I wandered down and tried to make conversation. He was elderly and hirsute, and he was fishing a squid bait with a brutally short rod and a line that would have kept you safe on Everest. As I recall, we had quite a long conversation without either of us really understanding anything the other said, thanks to my inadequate French and his Breton accent. Then suddenly he turned to the rod, gave a great shout and struck mightily, and I looked down to see a large and angry bass kicking at the water surface on the end of his line. '*C'est un bar, un bar!*' he shouted.

I could see immediately that he had a problem, because even his industrial-strength tackle was not capable of winching a bass that size fifteen feet up onto the jetty. Obviously realising this, the fisherman began to shout furious instructions at me, as the only other person within range, and began gesticulating with his spare arm between heaves on the rod. After an agonising few seconds it dawned on me that he wanted me to deploy a large and ancient drop net which lay with his gear on the concrete. I tried desperately to disentangle the cords which operated the net while he continued to shout, furious at my incompetence. Finally I freed the net and worked out how to lower it down without dropping it or tangling it again, he managed to steer the fish onto it, and between us we hauled the bass up on to the jetty. It looked to weigh between four and five pounds. I offered a congratulatory handshake, but the fisherman declined, seeming to regard the whole episode as a disaster and me as a total waste of *l'espace*, despite the happy ending.

I did not manage to catch a decent bass of my own until the Towy years were under way, some years later. There were regular weekend visits to my in-laws in Swansea, and in more active days Eurudd, my *tad-yn-gyfraith*, had been a keen angler. On the very first of these visits, when I was meeting them for the first time, I was scarcely allowed into the house before he ushered me back to the car and ordered me to drive. His daughter reacted with an amused smile, but Gwyneira, my *mam-yn-gyfraith*, seemed less happy. I thought we were perhaps popping down to the off-licence to top up his supplies of Tennants' Extra Strong, but by the time Eurudd indicated that we had reached our destination we were twenty miles away and out on the Gower coast. Here he pointed out various inlets where bass could be caught, and told me of one particular spot further on called Paviland Cave, which he knew to be a good spot for big ones. By the time we returned, dinner was on the point of ruin and my in-laws-to-be were (not unusually, I later realised) at war, but I had been given another vision of silver.

The south side of the Gower Peninsula is rich in bass country, with its granite coves and inlets, kelp beds and tide-washed reefs. The sea trout of the Towy were always the stronger pull, but there were only two kinds of opportunity to catch them, with the spinner or worm in falling high water by day and with the fly in settled low water by night, and more often than not conditions did not suggest that either would be successful. At such times, the bass served as a very satisfactory alternative.

I was beginning to learn about sea trout on the river bank, from men who were more than willing, during the long nights when the fish were not taking, to fill me in on the methods that worked when they were. I imagined I could learn about bass the same way, but it proved rather more difficult. Serious anglers seemed few and far between, for one thing. Bass fishermen are as restless and elusive as their quarry: here today for a couple of hours, gone tomorrow with their multipliers and bait-buckets to some other tide-swept reef, leaving nothing behind but their bootprints and a few fragments of sandeel.

And for another, they are a solitary breed. One rainy morning in a bay called Overton Mere I scrambled across half a mile of kelp-covered rock to make the acquaintance of a man I could see casting into the surf, thinking he might give me, as a newcomer to the game, some pointers. He ignored me totally, maintaining a convincing impression of an Easter Island statue until I ran out of ways of saying "Excuse me, can you tell me anything about the bass fishing round here?" and slunk off back the way I had come. I've had the same thing happen once or twice with carp fishermen. I suppose some people really do go fishing to get away from it all.

It was around this time that it started to dawn on me, very belatedly, that you don't catch bass by casting from rocky headlands into deep green abysses. A wonderful book I had just discovered called *Hooked On Bass*, by Mike Ladle and Alan Vaughan, had put me right on this. Bass, as you will know if you are a bass angler yourself, are not interested in deep, sheltered gullies; they leave them to the wrasse, pollack and conger. Bass like action – racing tide rips, surf-washed rocky platforms, sea-scoured rock pools; the troubled margins of the sea, in short, for it is here that their opportunistic hunting strategy pays off best. They are fish of dash and power, as unafraid of white water as my other great loves, the sea trout and the salmon.

This notion was vividly demonstrated one day during a low-tide visit to Worm's Head, which juts out like an ancient stranded sea-serpent at the southern end of Rhossili Beach on the tip of the Gower. I came upon a large rock pool not far above the low tide mark and was thrilled to see that it actually contained a shoal of twenty or so small bass, on the brink of release by the incoming tide. The explosion of silver as my shadow fell on the pool and the entire shoal poured through the flooding entrance and out into the ocean will stay with me for ever.

The best bait for bass, I learned from talking to a knowledgeable chap behind the counter at Capstan House, was crab, but not just any crab – it had to be soft edible crab, and preferably freshly caught, not frozen. I soon discovered that if the bass is the sea angler's silver prize, the fresh, soft edible crab is his gold. Find the gold, and the silver will follow relatively easily.

I drove down the evening before a big tide and hunted a stretch of rocky shore at dusk in a light drizzle for edible crabs. Finding edible crabs on the shore, big ones at least, is as testing and unpredictable as bass fishing itself, particularly when others have been there before you, and very few of those you do find will be soft. The job is punishingly hard on the back and the fingers. Sizeable ones are found only well down the shore close to the spring low-water mark, and it is rare to find one under a rock small enough to lift. However, I knew that I needed only one sizeable soft crab (you're not allowed to kill small edible crabs anyway) to make my trip viable, because it would make several baits. Without soft crab, I would be reduced to lure fishing; good, clean fun but vastly less productive, in my experience.

I hunted until it was nearly dark, and eventually unearthed a beautiful salmon-pink edible crab, four inches across and still soft from the moult. Cut up like a pie (they look rather like pies, with their crimped edges) and with the portions carefully bound to the hook with elastic thread, it would make at least four good baits.

I slept in the car, and woke at five to a grey Atlantic dawn. A short drive, a testing hike and a hairy climb later, I was sitting on a slab of ancient limestone at the foot of the cliffs of Paviland with the beginnings of a making tide mulling and swooshing at my feet. Sea slaters – huge, prehistoric woodlice – scurried into crannies, and an early-rising rock pipit watched me warily from the next outcrop.

My plan was to touch-leger as I had learned to do on rivers for chub and eels, using a light carbon fibre Daiwa Moonraker bass surfcaster, new and as yet unchristened. My weight was a lead bullet attached to the trace with a long link of fine nylon, so that if it got jammed between two rocks I could easily break it off without losing the rest of the rig. Mindful of my new realisation that bass prefer shallow water to deep, I didn't cast far but simply lobbed the bait about fifteen yards out into a swirling, shallow gully between slabs of rock, drew out some slack line and held it pinched between my left forefinger and thumb. I'd been told the best time was about an hour and a half into the tide.

For some time, nothing happened. The sea swelled up and started to swallow the rocks and I shifted my position a couple of times, mindful of the desirability of remaining within commuting distance of the mainland. Every twenty minutes or so I carefully wound in and changed the bait, mainly to reduce the risk of fishing through the golden hour with a bare hook, which would have been a tragic waste of opportunity. A couple of times there were the inevitable hangups, and very soon I was down to my last two baits.

At one point a large grey seal came and pondered my presence with ancient, unfathomable eyes from twenty yards away. I didn't think the seal would help my chances, but it wasn't long before it went on its way.

Nothing happened until, an hour and a half into the tide, I felt a gentle pluck and saw the rod tip nod, twice. Dead on time. I pointed the rod at the water and let the line run free. It drew quickly tight, and I struck.

Immediately I felt a great kicking weight, and knew I had hooked something important. I pumped and wound and heaved and very soon up it came, exactly as I had prayed, a great, swirling, spikey, black-and-silver bass. How rarely fishing goes so closely to plan! I scrabbled for the big round salmon net I had bought ready for this moment, and eventually, taking my life into my hands and getting extremely wet, I managed to draw the fish over it and haul the lot to safety.

I scrambled up the rocks, roaring my triumph to the seabirds, despatched the fish and gazed at it in joy. It went six pounds nine ounces, more than twice the size of any bass I had caught before.

After that I went back regularly to the cove. Whenever I managed to find a soft edible crab as bait, I seemed to get a bass or two. All too often the bait ran out within the first hour, mainly because other fish liked my soft edible crabs too; dogfish usually, and once a nice ling. When I couldn't find any edibles and was reduced to frozen sandeel or shop-bought peeler shore crab, the dogfish were all I caught. I didn't get another six-pounder, but I had several between two and three pounds and one that was nearly four. I soon discovered that float fishing is easier and more fun than legering; in fact I once had a bass seize my float, in the way that they will take plugs, and for a brief moment I thought it might even hang on long enough for me to land it.

In Swansea over the last weekend of August 1997, I was awoken very early on the Sunday morning by the sound of anxious discussion on the landing, and rose to find that we had lost the Princess of Wales. Once we'd all spent an hour or two in our dressing gowns in front of the television hearing about what seemed to have happened in the Pont de l'Alma tunnel, I felt the need for peace and fresh air and decided to go to the cove.

The forecast had been fine enough, but by the time I had

tackled up, a savage westerly had blown up. I was in one of those moods – end of season, death of Diana, back to work tomorrow – when I didn't really care what happened, whether or not I caught anything or how cold or wet I got. Unfortunately this insouciance gave me the nastiest moment I have ever had while sea fishing.

Standing on a rock separated from the main mass of the cliff by a narrow gully and casting a plug into the kelpy swell, I simply lost track of time. Some of the waves were crashing over my knees, but the water was warm and it seemed no more unpleasant than going overdepth in a pair of wellingtons. I felt so close to the ocean; untroubled by it, a part of it, even, though the plug was coming back draped with weed every cast and there seemed no chance whatsoever of any bass.

And then the sky seemed to darken to seaward and I looked up – and was struck dumb with horror. A vast, smooth, silent cliff of grey water was bearing down upon me from the middle distance like a mountain on roller skates. It filled the sky. It was the biggest wave I had ever seen, by a factor of at least three. I could not move, breathe or think. All I could do in the seconds that remained before the mountain engulfed me was cling to my little crag with both hands and knees and gasp in shock as the ocean struck.

How I was neither drowned nor dashed to pieces I have no idea, but the wave passed, the ocean drained away and I looked up and found that Wales was still there and I was still breathing. Naturally every inch of me was drenched, from my hair to my ankles. My tackle bag was upturned and its contents scattered, and as I climbed to my feet I spotted my bait can drifting out of reach in the backwash.

I turned, shaking, to leave, and realised with a second shock that the shallow gully I had so cheerfully hopped across on arrival had vanished. In its place was the Straits of Magellan. My little cleft between the rock slabs had become an open channel, my angling station an isolated tooth of offshore limestone.

I didn't, thank God, hesitate to think about the alternatives – well, there weren't any. The tide was in full flow and the wind still rising. With a strength fuelled by panic, I grasped my rod and jumped towards the rest of Wales as hard as I could. I hit the flank of the rock and my boots skidded back down into the water, but my fingers gripped the crest and slowly I managed to haul myself up to safety.

I didn't go back for a while, after that.

CHAPTER 10

A fence too far

Rain, midnight rain, nothing but the wild rain

Edward Thomas, 'Rain' (1916)

I t was hot. Much too hot to be drafting a quarterly profit forecast. Certainly too hot to fish. Even for sea trout. Even for the sewin of a wild Welsh river fining down to summer low, with the sandpipers calling to each other across the shingle banks and the solid splosh of the first moving fish of the evening...

I switched off the computer and drove to Wales. Well, it was Friday.

As I crossed the Severn Bridge, Bill Giles was rattling on about a warm, dry night with mist creeping in and the chance of a little drizzle towards dawn. But as I passed Eglwys Nunydd near Port Talbot, the lake which lies so close to the M4 that you can match the hatch through the windscreen, it began to rain. Quite soon after that it was chucking it down. The Towy doesn't normally let a little shower upset it, but this was proper rain. By the time I stopped to peer over at Llandeilo Bridge the river was stirring from its slumber, and by the time I reached Llangadog it was unmistakably in spate.

This was when I was still fairly new to sea trout, and completely new to catching them. I had read somewhere that a spate was not the best news if you were hoping to pull the trick off at night, but I have always believed in looking on the bright side. I calculated that if it stopped raining soon there was an excellent chance of a fish on the worm at first light.

As I finished the calculation, the sky flickered and brightened, and thunder began to roll around the hills. The heavy rain stopped, to make way for the very heavy rain.

So at ten, the time at which I had fondly pictured myself slipping into the silken waters of the Bridge Pool as gracefully as a supermodel into a Badedas bath, I was not standing in the Towy as planned. I was standing in the bar of the Castle Hotel in Llangadog, wrapped around the better part of my first pint of Felinfoel Bitter.

Robbie and Ken were following the same strategy, but the Castle was looking after them for the whole weekend, so they could afford to look upon time as their friend. They seemed to look upon me as their friend, too. They bought me a second pint of Felinfoel, so I bought them each one, and then they bought me another one, so the least I could do was... well, you get the picture.

It was Robbie's idea that we should, after all, go night fishing. Robbie was by this time talking more loudly than me or Ken and said he had caught a sea trout at night once before, so we were happy to let him be group expert. Robbie thought we should be fishing, so we went fishing. Ken, who was middle-aged and sensible, did not come.

Robbie said they had found a good pool, not the Bridge Pool but a better one, he explained, further upriver towards Llandovery. You could recognise it by an old deep-freeze which the river had dumped in the shallows at the top. So we drove to the bridge, unshipped our rods, climbed into our waders, stepped over the stile and set off.

It had been dark for a long time by now. It was not raining any more, but it must have only just stopped, because the grass was about as wet as it is possible for grass to be without actually being under water. Of course, we were wearing chest waders, so a little damp grass was not a problem. It seemed a long walk to the pool and there were a lot of barbed-wire fences to cross on the way. We found some of them by sight and others by touch. Sometimes finding them by touch hurt a bit, but not much, because of the Felinfoel Bitter. The rain seemed to be easing off and we were going to catch some sea trout, so what the heck.

We found the pool and the freezer and started to fish it (the pool, not the freezer). It looked quite big and fast for a sea-trout pool and not really distinguishable from the rest of the river, all of which looked (and sounded) big and fast by now. Robbie explained that in these conditions it was best to fish a big, dark fly, so we fished big, dark flies. We fished them right down the pool, by which time I was soaked to the waist. Up to the waist, not down to the waist. I think this was something to do with the barbed wire fences we had found by touch.

I didn't feel cold, though. This was partly because of the Felinfoel Bitter and partly because the current was swinging the line round so quickly that I was casting about 80 per cent of the time and fishing only about 20 per cent of the time.

At the tail of the pool Robbie wound in his fly and went off down to the next. I was about to follow him, but then something happened. I had a take.

Whatever I had hooked, it was big. A horribly powerful force began to tear line from the reel. I pulled back, but it made no difference – the creature behind the force was going back to the sea, regardless of any view I might hold on the matter.

I pumped and heaved until the rod tip was very nearly touching the reel. The pressure stopped suddenly. I wound in. The fly had gone.

Down at the next pool, Robbie looked shorter than I remembered him. As I got closer I found that this was because he was sitting down. I couldn't see if his legs were wet like mine as they were under water, but his hair was certainly wet. It did not really suit him.

"I've just gone in" he said. "This sheep came past. It was still twitching, so I tried to grab it, but I've gone in over my waders."

So I didn't tell Robbie that I had hooked a big fish. I did think of telling him that I had seen the sheep and had tried to save it by casting over it, but had lost it at the net. In the end I don't think I mentioned it at all, as its choice of a size eight Black Squirrel seemed rather academic.

We fished on for quite a while, but we did not catch any sea trout, or anything else, apart from a number of small branches and a fresh-run blue plastic fertiliser bag. Robbie explained that although the conditions were otherwise pretty encouraging, sea trout do not take well when there is a full moon. I looked to see if there was indeed a full moon, but there was no sign of one. It was raining quite hard again by now, which would of course explain this.

So we wound in and walked back. Actually, 'walked' is the wrong word. Stumbled, staggered, floundered, limped – any of those would be closer. We had drunk a lot of Felinfoel Bitter, but not enough to last us this long, and it was raining almost as hard as it had been when the adventure had started.

We did not really know where we were, so we navigated our way back downriver by dead reckoning – Robbie explained that this was the best way if you were lost in unfamiliar territory at night. We found more barbed-wire fences at various stages of maturity, some of them at chest level, some at thigh level and some only at ankle level. We found hardly any of them by sight and nearly all of them by touch.

Now I should explain that one of the Towy's most interesting features is the way it meanders. If you think your river meanders, you ought to see the Towy. It meanders for England, or rather for Wales. It meanders so much that in places you can walk all day along its banks and still throw a stone into the pool where you started. Its meanders, and the resulting oxbow lakes, are among the most fascinating features of the geography of this part of the Dyffryn Tywi.

But to be honest, I did not feel very interested in geography by the time we had been stumbling, staggering, floundering and limping along for forty-five minutes or so. By that time we had both lost our hats, my fishing torch had gone and Robbie had torn his net beyond repair. And any remaining interest I had felt in geography disappeared completely when I tripped over a familiar-looking piece of bank and saw the freezer again.

Sleeping through the night on a riverbank has a certain romantic appeal, but not when you are soaked from head to foot and do not have a hat between you, so we had another go at getting home.

We were very tired indeed by the time we had crossed all the barbed-wire fences again, as well as some new ones, and found the main A40 (I have often grumbled to myself since, when night fishing, about the whine of the all-night traffic on the A40, but that night it would have been elected Most Popular Trunk Road In Great Britain without a dissenting voice). I thought that was why I hadn't heard Robbie explain anything for so long, until I waited for him and realised that he must have gone a different way. I do hope he got home safely – it's been more than thirty years, so he ought to have made it by now.

I walked west through the rain along the A40 until I came to the road that led back to Llangadog and the place where I had left the car.

The next morning I went to look at the river, and found it immediately. It was the size of the St Lawrence Seaway. It took me longer to find my torch and hat (the torch was still working, but not the hat – it would have been a tight fit for a water vole).

I turned the car round and drove back to England. At first I did not feel I would bother to fish for sea trout again, even the sewin of a wild Welsh river fining down to summer low, but I have always believed in looking on the bright side.

Adapted from an article first published in Salmon, Trout & Sea Trout *magazine*

CHAPTER 11

Potted sewin

Fish (fly-replete, in depth of June
Dawdling away their wat'ry noon)...

Rupert Brooke, 'Heaven'

Y ou couldn't pop over to Cardiff this afternoon and attend a briefing meeting about the marketing plan for the new development, could you? Sorry it's such short notice," said my boss's voice on the phone.

Cardiff. Wales. Towy. Sea trout.

"No problem, Philip," I replied, careful to keep my voice flat and professional. "Anything for a client."

I was thinking fast. It would be an inexcusable waste of petrol to drive from Bristol all the way to Cardiff and not take a look at my river, which couldn't be more than sixty miles or so further on. I might even be able to fish, if I could get a ticket at such short notice. I wasn't expecting to actually *catch* anything, of course. Not after five years of almost entirely blank days and nights. Perhaps when the rains came there might be a chance, but right now we were in the middle of a drought. It would just be nice to take a look at the river, to recce a new pool or two, to rub shoulders with other anglers and listen to their tales of success in decades gone by.

I left Cardiff in the evening rush hour and motored west along the M4 through the commuters and weekend holiday traffic. Then I turned north at Cross Hands up through Ammanford to the club stretch of the Towy which had been the focus of my campaign for the past season. I had been planning to change from my business clothes into my fishing gear in the layby next to the river at Llyshendy, but there were cars there before me and people around, so I changed in the field instead. I noticed that the tailgate of one of the cars was open and an old man in black waders was sitting under it, drinking from a flask.

"Come for the night, have you," he said, making it a statement.

"Thought I'd give it a go," I said. "Better than sitting at home watching telly."

"Personally I would choose the television," he said.

"Not so good, then?"

He looked across towards the river and made a long-drawn out noise of mingled disgust and grief, like a man surveying a battlefield the morning after.

"I remember the time when you could come down to this pool *hyur"* – he waved a hand towards the neighbouring loop of river – "and 'ave half a dozen sewin on the bank before midnight. Big ones, mind! Double figures, some. Now you'd be lucky to get half a dozen in a season."

"The fish just aren't there, then?"

"The fish are not there," he said emphatically, and then conceded: "A few. Potted fish. Maybe in August, if it rains, we might have a chance. If it dun't rain, you can forget it."

I started to tackle up, trying not to insult him by displaying any sign of confidence or enthusiasm. After what he had said, I found this quite easy.

When he had driven off, I picked up my rods, one loaded with a floating line, the other with a sink-tip, shouldered my bag and net and set off on the trek to my chosen pool. The sun had sunk below the tree line, but the earth was still radiating heat like a three-bar electric fire and the newly-harvested hay had left a powerful, yeasty smell behind. My waders contributed to the heat from the inside and a plague of horseflies added to it from the outside, so by the time I reached the Stones I was in a muck sweat and not in the best of tempers.

My mood was not helped by the fact that as I rounded each bend, I saw that the line that marked the division between field-edge and river was punctuated at regular intervals by anglers' heads; three on the Baskets, two on Banc y Berllan, two on the Car Pool and now, on the Stones, the best pool of all, four. Four anglers where there was room for no more than two! I had expected to be allowed to suffer the expected blank night in private, but at this rate I would be lucky to get my fly into the water at all.

I dumped my gear at the top of the bank just below the bottom of the pool, by the pot, and started to cool off.

Now the sun had gone, it was turning into a pleasant evening. The sand martins were having a party with the olives and sedges and a pair of grey wagtails were sorting through the leftovers. I sat for a while, cooling off. I remembered Falkus' advice: *'Provided the fish are in the river only one excuse is valid – that the river is in spate and the water coloured. No other conditions preclude the catching of fish at night.'* I took heart, slightly.

The Stones is a most inviting pool. There's a fast shallow stretch above it, then the current whangs across to the far side and sculpts out a secretive-looking eddy under the bank before opening up into a big, deep pot which can be relied upon to hold a salmon in the last few weeks of the season. Below the pot the pool runs deep and straight under trees for more than a hundred yards, shallowing gradually towards a shingled, weedy tail. All along the far side alders and willows hang low, and at the water's edge under them lie the massive stone blocks that give the pool its name, put there to prevent the river from undermining the bed of the railway track above. The water under the trees is dark and steady and always, in high summer, it holds big sewin. Sometimes people catch them.

Not tonight, of course – far too low. I hadn't been sitting there long when I heard a duet of reel checks from above and realised that the two anglers at my end of the pool had reached the same conclusion. First one, then the other, lumbered up on to the bank, now in total darkness, and plodded towards me.

"From away, are you?" said the first. "Not local?" I wasn't sure how he could tell this in the dark; do English anglers smell different?

"I've driven from Bristol."

"Ah. This feller's from Bristol, Ron. How long that take you, then?"

"Hour and a half."

"Hour and a half. Well you've wasted your time tonight, my friend, there's not a takeable fish in the river."

"Might be a chance later when it cools down a bit," I offered.

"Ah, when it cools *down*. September, you mean?" They both agreed this was a good joke and laughed. I tried to put on a cheerful smile, pretending they were laughing with me, but they were not.

They plodded off, and I weighed the situation up. The men downstream hadn't apparently objected to having those two anglers above them, so presumably they wouldn't mind me in their place. I pulled up my waders, unshipped the fly from the keeper ring, worked out a few yards of line and slid into the water at my feet. I could do this easily enough in the dark; I knew the pool well, even though I'd never taken a sizeable sea trout there, or of course anywhere else.

I had only been in the water a few seconds when there came from downstream that little splurring noise a big sewin makes with its tail to let you know it has lift-off, followed half a second later by the almighty 'spaloosh' that makes newcomers to the river rush to check on their host, thinking he has fallen in.

"Hey Tommy bach, that's a big bugger!" said a voice from somewhere beyond the splash. "Better cover 'im."

There was a short interval, and then without warning I heard the bushes part and a large, dark shape crashed into the water immediately in front of me.

"Bloody hell!" said the voice, much closer this time. "Sorry boy, didn't know you were there."

"No, my fault," I said. "Should have checked before I went in."

"You carry on, my friend, you won't bother us. There's not a catchable sewin in the river anyway, if you ask me. Need some fresh water to bring 'em up. Last year we didn't get one till October, did we, Cliff? And then it was a salmon."

This seemed unnecessarily pessimistic, even to me.

"What about the one we just heard?"

"Potted fish. Bin yur for weeks. Never catch 'em when they do that. Still, beats sittin' at home watchin' the telly, innit?"

But it wasn't long before they too packed up. They wound in their lines and plodded past me back to the road, wishing me success and promising me failure almost in the same sentence.

I fished on for a bit, feeling sure, now the locals had voted with their feet, that my quest wasn't just unlikely; it was absurd. I thought of pubs and parties, of girls and music, of a Horizon special about the universe I was missing on TV, of my bed; particularly of my bed.

But I didn't pack up. I had come a long way. To reel in and go home seemed so – defeatist. And it had turned into a lovely velvet-soft night. I just kept on wading and casting, fingers numb, shoulders creaking, back slowly stiffening up. On the Towy flowed around me, gurgling faintly in the dark, and every once in a while there would come another great splosh of potted sewin.

Again and again I shuffled a pace further downstream, inched back the line through my fingers until I felt the belly, hoiked the rod up into a steeple cast and punched it back under the trees. I fished down that pool once, twice, three times. I became an automaton, unthinking, uncaring, unfeeling; unhinged, probably.

Some time around two in the morning, I noticed that I couldn't see the lights of Llandeilo any more; I felt uneasy about that. Uneasy, and a bit lonely. The reason I couldn't see them was that it had started to rain.

What a fiasco. You drive a hundred miles, you walk for twenty minutes carrying half a tackle shop, you queue for the only decent pool, and then it rains. Well thank you very much. A couple more casts and then...

And that's when it happened. One moment I was minding my own business, fingering back the line for another cast, and the next something had sandbagged the rod and nearly snatched it from my hand, so utterly without warning that for an instant I dropped the line. I grabbed the rod with both hands instead, lifted, and felt an unspeakably violent force going the other way.

I don't remember the details; it was all far too much of a shock. The reel must have snarled, the line would have hissed, certainly my left leg will have trembled. Yet somehow, after a great deal of splashing by both me and the fish, one of us landed the other, carried it to the bank and laid it out. It really was a sea trout, a proper slab of a fish, almost fresh run, the thing I'd been after all these years, and there it was lying before me in the dew. It was indescribably beautiful.

I extracted the two-inch sunk lure it had taken and pocketed it to show it to my grandchildren, should I ever have any. Then I dug out my spring balance; eight pounds one ounce.

As for me, I weighed nothing at all. I danced back into the river, fished on for a bit, and then when nothing else had happened for an hour or so I wound in and skipped the three fields back to the car through the rain. The grass was very wet by now and as I hadn't brought a coat, so was I, but I could not possibly have cared less.

All the way back to Cross Hands and the A48, the road was hopping with toads joyfully soaking up the rain after the long drought. I knew just how they felt.

CHAPTER 12

Nuts in Mayo

Watched the Galway salmon run
Like silver dancing, darting in the sun...
I stood by your Atlantic sea
And sang a song for Ireland.

Phil Colclough, 'Song For Ireland'

T im's message on the answering machine started it. The gang were planning a week in early summer on the Moy, but Dave might have to drop out through pressure of work. If so, would I like to take his place? Tim had already told me, in unnecessary detail, about the fifty-four salmon to 13lb they had taken on the last trip, and this year they were going at a better time.

I said yes, obviously. Over the next few weeks, when I wasn't thinking about Ireland, I was thinking about Dave, and hoping his business was going really well.

Tim, Roly, Tony, Paul, Sean, Chris Leat and I met up at Severn Bridge Services on the last Saturday evening in May and drove in a three-car convoy down the M4 to catch the night ferry to Rosslare. The boat had a lot of beer, and we had to plan the downfall of a lot of fish, so by the time we got to our cabins it was very nearly time to get up again. I wasn't able to take a nap en route (even in Ireland you're not supposed to drive while you're asleep), so by the time we got to Ballina in the early evening I was looking forward to getting my head down for an hour or two before meeting up to plan the following day's fishing.

We claimed our rooms and I called to Tim to ask what time he wanted the alarm set for. There was no reply. Tim was down in the yard with the others, tackling up. They couldn't wait till tomorrow, so Paul Wade, our guide, was taking us to fish the River Deel, which flows from Lough Conn into the Moy not far from Ballina.

The Deel is not a big river. When Tony asked Paul if he would need his new Sage fifteen-footer, Paul (when he had stopped laughing) said that he wouldn't even need a fifteen-foot line. We had a lot of fun fishing the Deel, but we caught nothing apart from one or two tiny trout. It was dull and chilly and what fly life we saw was restricted to a few olives.

On the way back we had a good look at the Moy. It seemed rather industrialised for a salmon river. Though the water was deep, clear and fast, the main town beats were only a couple of hundred yards long and boxed in by stone walls and concrete embankments. Along the Cathedral beat rocky groynes had been constructed every twenty-five yards or so, and on each of these stood an angler. To make sure no one hogs a productive spot, you're supposed to move down one groyne every hour – a bell sounds to give the signal.

Below the Cathedral is the Ridge Pool, which is even more famous and even more industrialised; a massive office block development was under way on the left bank and anglers were queuing up in the shadow of a 150-foot crane for their turn to get in at the top of the pool. We watched them for a while, studying their technique through binoculars. They all seemed to be dressed to kill in Gore-Tex and Neoprene, but there was more dressing than killing; most of them could have done with a casting lesson or two. The ones who could reach the deep channel under the wall on the right bank, where Paul said the fish would be running through, were doing best. Every so often one of them would raise his rod and we would see white water and silver. We didn't know yet whether we'd be fishing the Ridge Pool, but we certainly hoped so.

We met up with Paul Wade in Healey's Bar and while we began our assault on the Guinness, he told us about the fishing. Healey's is a pub one side and a tackle shop the other, so Sean ordered seven pints of Guinness and a hundred yards of 12lb nylon and I put in for half a dozen Ally's Shrimps tied on no. 10 doubles and seven bags of smoky bacon crisps. As we listened to Paul, the rest of the pub's clientèle joined in with their own little nuggets of local knowledge. In Ballina, everyone is either an angler or an angling supporter.

We were anxious to find out where we would be fishing and when, so Paul explained his plan for the week. It was fiendishly simple; we would see how things turned out. We understood this to mean that Paul, using his considerable local knowledge and numerous contacts, would keep us abreast of opportunities and developments on a day-by-day basis and each day we would decide whether to do what he suggested or something else.

We drank a lot of Guinness that night. It's true, of course, that the Guinness tastes better in Ireland; everything tastes better in Ireland, when you're on a fishing holiday with your buddies.

On Monday, Tim, Sean, Roly and Paul Elliott went out on Lough Conn while Paul Wade took Tony, Chris and me up to Foxford to learn the art of bubble-fly-fishing. You rig up a three-fly leader on spinning tackle, except that where the point fly ought to be you tie on a bubble float. You cast square across the current, then wind it back.

The Moy was a foot or two up and coloured and as I listened to Paul's instructions I was looking discreetly around for some nice soft earth where I could dig some worms after he'd gone. I didn't want to argue with the guide, but I couldn't believe anything would beat the worm on a day like this.

I should have known better. I cast the bubble float out across the river and wound it back and instantly I caught a grilse. It was the smallest one I'd ever seen, two pounds at the outside, but undeniably it was a grilse. I held it up to show Tony and Chris and there was a lot of whooping and back-slapping and hand-shaking. Then we all cast in side by side, racing each other for the next fish.

We went on casting for eight hours without another take. We tried the worm, we tried the spinner, we tried the sunk fly. The river was rising slightly, which may have explained it.

Back at the holiday flats, we met up with the Conn team. Sean, Roly and Paul had blanked, but Tim, fishing with dabblers and mayfly patterns, had taken four of the most beautiful trout you ever saw, heavily marked and weighing between 2lb and 3lb 13oz. Tim had done this sort of fishing before, of course. We were waiting for him to lecture to us about how he'd done it so we could have fun knocking him off his pedestal, but he was too cunning for us, as he had been too cunning for the trout.

That night we went to a bigger pub and had a slap-up meal; that was Tim's idea. We drank a lot of Guinness, and Tim paid; that was our idea.

On the Tuesday it was time for Tony, Chris and me to fish Conn while the others made their débuts on the Ridge and Cathedral pools. We set out with high hopes after Tim's success, but the wind turned north, May became March and not even the skills of John Gallagher, the boatman, could bring the trout up from the depths.

Conn was so beautiful, though, that it gave us a day to remember just the same. It was huge, deep, dark and wild, with innumerable little rocky inlets, islets and promontories, all constructed on an impressive scale from limestone rocks and slabs and tufted with willow and alder scrub. There were scoters, mergansers and oystercatchers, so tame (the whole lake is a reserve) that you can study them without binoculars. It made the reservoirs I was used to back home in England seem small, muddy and suburban.

We asked how deep the lake was, and John related how two men from the North had come up a few weeks previously for a spot of illicit eel fishing at night. The net had got snagged on a rock in fifty feet of water. They revved up the outboard to yank it free and the boat stood on its stern and went down like a breeze block. One of the men had still not been found.

After such a long, fruitless day, I was not as sorry as I should have been when we got back to find that the other party had also blanked. Tim, using my double-hander, had made contact with a good salmon on the Cathedral Pool and after a few tense moments, lost it again. We all told him how sorry we were.

On the Wednesday we fished the upper beats of the Ballina town water, Ash Tree and Spring Wells, and took turns to go out in a boat. The boatman was called Jacky, and he knew a thing or two about salmon fishing. He was carrying a priest the size of a table leg; an encouraging sign, I felt, and said as much to Paul Wade.

"Whatever you do, if you get a pull, don't strike" said Paul. "That's what the priest is for. One of the boys kept striking last year, and every time he did it Jacky hit him on the arm with the priest until he got the message."

But by the end of the day, with only two more Lilliputian grilse to our credit, we would all have given our right arms to feel Jacky's priest hitting, well, our right arms. It seemed the Moy was 'off'. So on Thursday, Paul announced that it was time for something completely different. We were going to the seaside, to fish for sea trout.

We dressed to the teeth, loaded ourselves with rods and trudged through gorse and over sand dunes and along a great expanse of deserted beach until we reached Ross Point and the mouth of a little river called the Cloonaghmore which flows out into Killala Bay. We were all very hot by the time we got there, and I for one felt a bit daft sitting on one of the most beautiful beaches in Ireland on a glorious June afternoon dressed up like a lifeboatman.

Again, Paul told us what to do. You tackle up as if you are clear-water worming, with a long, light rod and fine mono, and attach a frozen sandeel by the head to a small bait hook. Then you work the bait out (strictly no floats or weights) and feel carefully for the takes.

I don't think I've ever been happier with a rod than I was that afternoon, once I had cooled off and dumped most of my gear on the sand to worry about later. We spread out, wading deeper and deeper into the swell in chest waders and T-shirts and working our baits along and across the making tide.

I was using my worming rod, an old 11ft Daiwa designed for river fishing for barbel and chub. It wasn't long before I felt a gentle tapping on the tip and struck to find not only that I had hooked a lively fish but that it was, indeed, a sea trout – not big, not much over a pound, but sea-bright and loaded with lice (too many lice, actually. Half a dozen indicate that a fish is fresh, but thirty or forty, as this one had, is too much for a small sea trout's health, and tells you something is wrong).

We didn't catch a lot of fish – about a dozen sea trout to a couple of pounds or so – but the scenery and the rolling tide and the salt sea air and the sight of Tim going in over the top of his waders brought joy to all our hearts.

While the rest of us fished a moving bait in mid water, Chris Leat decided to try laying on in a deep gully, and soon enjoyed his first success of the week, a fine spider crab that stripped off several inches of line before he was able to subdue it.

As the tide started to make in earnest, I spotted the shiny football-head of a seal bobbing far out beyond the breakers. And then something much more remarkable – a dolphin rolled, shining black against the bright water, no more than a hundred yards out (I know now that it was probably a Bottlenose). Then another, and another, until it was clear we had a school of the things. They looked huge and exotic. Too huge and exotic for Roly, who lost valuable fishing time by running backwards up the beach, until someone went after him to explain the difference between dolphins and sharks.

We were on the river again on the Friday and Tony, Chris and I fished the Cathedral Pool on the only day of the week when it didn't produce a single salmon. Still that north wind. So in the evening Paul Wade marched us out to Bullockpark on the other side of the bay and we caught some more sea trout in a weedy tide rip. This was good enough sport for all of us except Chris Leat. By putting plenty of lead on his line he got his sandeel well down past the sea trout and landed more fine crabs, of several species.

On the last day, I made a terrible mistake. I accepted a lift in Roly's Volvo. That is not to say that Roly is a bad driver or that I dislike Volvos, just that from my point of view his had an important drawback; it didn't have my tackle in it. In the moments between accepting a lift with him and leaving Ballina, I scrabbled around to transfer the gear I thought I would need for Conn. I managed to remember everything except my camera, my hat, my boots, my packed lunch, my fly box and most of my nylon. I also forgot my thermometer, but that was OK because Roly had one. Actually Roly had several; he is by far the best-equipped angler I have ever met. I know anglers who carry a vice and an assortment of fly-tying materials in the car in case they are called upon to simulate an unusual insect, but Roly carries an entire fly-tying workshop, complete with bench and lights. If it was any bigger, it would qualify for an EC grant.

My thermometer is made of plastic and was £1.49 from Boots. Roly's was rather different. It consisted of a little sensor on the end of a length of fine cable, attached to a plastic box with a digital display which could give the temperature to an accuracy of a tenth of a degree and download the details to a computer; commonplace now perhaps, but this was in 1998.

I say 'was' and 'could' because when I was stepping out of the boat on to an island for our picnic lunch I clipped the thermometer with my heel and sent it flying into the water, killing it instantly. I have already apologised profoundly several times to Roly, but if he should ever read this, I really am sorry, mate.

Anyway, about the fishing. By comparison with our Tuesday outing, the conditions were much more promising – it was a soft, bright day, though still a trifle chilly. We chugged up the lake and into a calm, shallow bay and started to see good rises to mayfly. It was clear the browns knew what boats were for, though, because they left a thirty-yard no-go area all round ours, even with the engine switched off, something you don't get very often with reservoir rainbows. We just kept drifting quietly, John steering with an oar, the two of us double-hauling as delicately as we could towards the horizon.

At last, on the stroke of midday (if such precision is appropriate in Ireland), the water around the claret dabbler I had borrowed from Sean opened up and the leader snaked off down into the depths below.

It was a good fish, and it stayed deep for quite a while. John held the boat and whispered encouragement, I kept the pressure on and slowly, grudgingly, the fish came to John's waiting net. It was the most beautiful lake trout I had ever seen, hard-muscled and densely spotted, and it weighed three and a half pounds; I wished for that camera.

That was the only chance we had. Soon afterwards the wind got up, the calendar went back to March again and the show was over for the day. That night, we drank a lot of Guinness, and I paid, paying particular attention to Roly's glass.

We were going to go back. But families and work somehow got in the way and then, the following year, Tim phoned to say that Paul Wade had died (we'd suspected he was ill, but we didn't realise how serious it was) and they had scattered his ashes on Conn. And then, four years after that, on the eve of a pike-fishing trip to Chew Valley Lake, Paul Elliott died too, utterly without warning. He was 52.

So if you can dedicate a chapter to someone, this one is dedicated to the two Pauls.

CHAPTER 13

A midsummer night stream

There is nothing, nothing in the whole sport of fishing so enchanting as a sea trout spate river in the drowsy dusk of a warm summer evening.

Hugh Falkus, 'Sea Trout Fishing'

It's the eyes that go first, I find, usually some time around two in the morning; odd, when you consider how little they have to do at night. I could wade ashore and try to revive them by napping on the bank for a few minutes, but that would be an unacceptable waste of fishing time, and I know I would wake with cold bones and a deathly need for true sleep. So instead I stand there in mid-river with eyes closed and teeth gritted, like a vampire in an upright coffin, and keep right on fishing. I have found it possible to carry on casting and retrieving like this for some time, poised in the simulation of sleep. It is best not to let these little trances last more than a few minutes, for you can lose track of which way is up and stumble, shipping a legfull of water, or perhaps actually pass out and topple unconscious into the river, never to be seen by your loved ones, or anyone else, again.

The back will also be registering a protest by now, because deep wading does not allow any respite from an erect stance, and weak, office-chair-mollycoddled lower back muscles do not cope well with hours of aquatic sentry duty. The shoulders will be creaking, from casting every thirty seconds without a break for three hours, and the fingers, softened by constant contact with the water and frayed by knots and hooks, are beginning to feel a little sore. The legs usually hold up pretty well from the structural point of view, but if the river still has a spring chill to it the water's icy grip will slowly strangle most of the feeling from them.

On those rare carnival nights when the fish take eagerly, sleep and the cloak of night are cast aside and forgotten. You remain the bright-eyed hunter, stalking the prey with all five wits ablaze, until happy exhaustion hits like a tranquilliser dart some time in the opening stages of the next day. But sea-trout nights rarely rush past like this. For all your determination to fight an active and varied campaign and take the battle to the fish, most of them turn into slow, passive affairs, long, cold, stiff, enduring, waiting-for-Godot vigils; more like vertical carp fishing.

This is how a typical night unfolds: you lumber down to the pool at sundown as clumsy and impatient as a bullock, cursing the weight of the coat and sweaters you have had to lug across the fields as insurance against the chill of the still far-off small hours. With eager fingers rods are assembled, reels mounted, lines threaded, flies and leaders fumbled together. Then, when everything is ready, all the urgency melts away, stupidly redundant. There is nothing to do now but sit on the top of the bank swinging your wadered legs, watching the darkening river and wondering how the night will go.

As the light fades bat-shadows dart and flicker, badgers rustle in the wood, a heron cranks past on its way to roost. Moorhens squabble and splash in temper over who's sleeping on whose side of the bed. Distant farm dogs bark in relay, and are stilled by their distant owners. The night begins to close in, scented and thrilling, everything a sea-trout night should be; and slowly, oh so slowly, the water in front of you fades to the desired shade of pale black.

At last, as the first stars prick forth overhead, you pick your way down the bank, step out into the head of the pool and start to work out line. And here's a thing; very often, so often you come to expect it, you get a take almost immediately. Back you snap on the instant with fighter-pilot reactions, but this fish never had hold of the fly properly in the first place; a finnock, probably. It's unlikely, this early in the night, to have been large. So nothing yet has been lost and nothing important missed, and all is to play for; at this point everything, on this perfect night, is still possible.

Full of confidence, with all the night to go and a mile of river to yourself, you flick and swish your way down the pool. When you look back at it afterwards, it is hard to see how you could done have done this part any better. Without a stumble, with hardly a false cast in either sense, you feel your fly through the water, down under the shadow of the alder grove to the high bank where the sand martins nest. On you cast and on, past the dead willow and into the corner by the fence-post where the current begins to pick up speed and you start to hear the chatter of the run-out thirty yards below; a fellow angler left his coat on that post once and you nearly died of shock when you looked up to see its silhouette looking down at you.

Again and again you cast out and finger back the line, and at each moment of each draw you are willing the tackle to shoot out tight with the sweet, heavy shock of a fish. But it refuses to happen. At last, when you have covered all the taking water, you reel in and wade slowly and quietly back inshore to try it through again, perhaps with a different fly or a faster-sinking line. And so the night trickles on, with the black river tiptoeing past and meteors flickering out overhead like spent matches; and perhaps once in a while, the splutter and crash as a big sea trout leaps from a willowed pool. Until, finally, the sky pales in the east and you know that despite all your preparations and all your hopes, you will once again be going home fishless.

But sometimes there is a night which does not end like this.

It was July, and we were already past the peak of a season which had so far put barely a mark in the fishing diary. I had begun it in great hope, having enjoyed something of an *annus mirabilis* the previous year with a dozen sizeable sewin and a brace of late but lovely salmon. This year, apart from one or two finnock, I had failed to put a single fish on the bank. In the hope that a change of scenery would do the trick, I had transferred my attention to a beat lower down the river on the Golden Grove fishery, one I had not ventured to fish before because I had thought it too expensive.

The beat looked wonderful; two miles of quietly winding river, flowing between pasture and woodland down to Cilsane Bridge. It had the luxury of a couple of designated parking areas, and the barbed-wire fences had been fitted with crossing points. A lot of walking would be involved, but in every other respect access was easy.

Having completed a preliminary reconnoitre and tucked away an early supper in the pub, I ambled down to the water's edge, dropped my tackle in the grass and surveyed the river. It was swollen by perhaps nine inches compared with typical summer low, the season having been generally wet so far, but there was not a trace of colour. The temperature was comfortably in the high teens and the water shimmered with tiny life; fry teemed in the margins, numberless parr were slashing at olives in the riffles, and sand martins and swallows were fighting an airborne battle for the leftovers. Surely these cheerful waters would part with a fish or two later, once the valley was cloaked in dark.

I put up a small silvery fly on a floating line and started perusing the river's faster passages. I was not really expecting engagement yet, just limbering up, getting my eye in for the main assault that would come at nightfall.

Slowly early evening became late evening, and late evening faded to dusk. I went on flicking my flies into the dubs and runs and creases until I came to a little beach, half sand, half mud, below a grassy bank; a cattle drink. The cattle drink had a friendly air about it, as indeed did the cattle still standing in it, but what I liked most about the place was that the water opened out below into a deep and beautiful pool. The pool was so long that I could not see the other end of it, and it was lined on both sides by overhanging ashes, alders and willows. This, surely, would be the kingdom of the sea trout.

I was determined to tackle it with care. I put up a sinking line loaded with a two-inch black-and-silver lure and sat down to wait for the dark. In this I was not disappointed. There was no moon and the sky was overcast, so by half past ten it was so black I had to put a finger in the river to find it. An otter came past me at one point; I know this only because I heard the snort and saw the swirl as it performed a *volte face* inches from my waders.

Around midnight I looked back upstream whence I had come and saw something very curious – two wavering points of light just above the water surface, tracking steadily out from the near bank towards the far one. I could not imagine what they were – giant glow worms? Aliens? Until a zephyr of night air carried voices towards me across the water and I realised that they were the torches of two anglers filing back to their cars, parked up in the lane on the far side of the river; I had not been alone on the beat after all.

I watched the little lights waver up the bank and bob away across the meadow and after a few minutes, heard the whump-whumpety-whump of car doors and the sound of engines being fired up.

It was not long after that when the first fish jumped.

I had heard big sea trout jump before of course, so I was used to that moment when you think a cow has gone in and you're going to have to call the farmer to drag it out with his tractor. Even so, you never quite get used to the recklessness of the splash, particularly when the sound is amplified by a still night.

Now when sea trout jump like this, it does not mean you are going to catch one. It does, however, show that there are fish in the pool with you, and as an antidote to drowsiness, it is much more effective than caffeine tablets.

I worked the fly carefully down, full of anticipation, towards the place where I had heard the fish jump. It soon became clear that I was not going to reach it, however. With every pace I took the water was getting deeper and the bank behind more overgrown, until very soon I was standing in a tunnel of overhanging willows, the water lapping at the kangaroo pouch on my waders.

This was turning into quite a dilemma. The sploshes were now coming quite regularly. First you would hear a little splurring noise, like the propeller of a toy motorboat when you lift it from the bath, then about a third of a second later there would come another great bovine splash from the invisible recesses of the invisible pool.

I went on wading, inch by inch, towards the sound. I waded until I was standing on tiptoe, the water was covering the logo on my chest waders and the fly box in my wading jacket was several inches under water. I waded until the elbows of my sweater were trailing in the current like wet socks. I was a polite cough away from shipping forty gallons of river water, but I didn't care, because I was quite happy to risk drowning for a chance at one of those fish.

I began to double-haul with increasing ferocity, the fly whizzing further and further downstream towards the unseen heart of the pool. Then I started stripping off line and letting the whole shooting match drift on down until the fly was trailing well beyond casting range.

It was all hopeless, of course; not a sniff.

I teetered with infinite care back up into comfortable water, clambered up through the willow roots, regained the bank, leaned my rod against a bush and twisted the top from a bottle of ginger beer. It was a relief to flop down on to the grass and feel my abused back muscles beginning to recover. I pressed the light button on my watch; one o'clock. Still early. The Towy slid past in front of me, silent apart from a faint trickle from the point upstream where the Cilsane Brook joins the main river. And still, far below in the blackness, those great fish were tombstoning into the water.

When you're trying to solve a fishing conundrum, nothing aids the brain cells like putting the rod down for a few minutes. As I sat in the dew and mulled over the situation, I began to realise that I was missing the point. These sewin were not going to take a fly even if I could get one to them. They would be resident fish, long-term stayers which had been there for weeks. My chance would come when – if – one of them went for a midnight stroll, as sea trout do. A wandering fish would be less likely to show, but much more likely to take. And until they wandered I wouldn't be able to reach them in any case.

So I gave up trying to cast to those impossible monsters. Instead I resolved to fish carefully on from where I had started at the top of the pool, in the hope that one of them, at some point, would venture out of its lair and come questing upstream away from the sanctuary and towards my fly.

So I went back up to the neck and started fishing down

from the run-in again, just as I had at dusk. Thinking a smaller fly might help – as it often does on a slow night – I dropped a size, to a one-and-a-half inch Waddington.

The sploshes went on, but some time around half past one there came one with a difference. It was a boil, rather than a watery crash, and it was not down in the belly of the impossible pool; it was just below the end of the run-in, almost within range of where I was standing.

I stayed calm. I cast quietly towards it, shuffled down a pace and cast again.

Firmly, without fuss, the fish took.

There was some slow, puzzled kicking, of the sort you often get when a big sea trout is first hooked, and then it woke up.

I have grappled with a few decent fish over the years, but never before or since have I experienced anything like the run that happened next. The rod bent in a hoop, and the reel, which was an ageing multiplier with a rather noisy check, screamed in shock. The sinker flashed through the rings like the TGV going through the Simplon Tunnel, and I felt the backing knot fly out after it.

I remember only one thought; that interesting as all this was, it was only distantly related to the business of catching big sea trout, because there was no question of this particular fish ever coming anywhere near me again. Another few milliseconds and it would have broken my tackle like candyfloss and be halfway to Carmarthen, leaving me a fishless, flyless, helpless spectator.

But then the fish stopped; I heard it boil massively on the surface. A full 70 yards away in the heart of an untamable pool and with most of my backing out, but in mid-river and with no obvious snags to intervene… perhaps the impossible was merely very unlikely. I pumped and wound, with trembling hands. Very slowly, the fish came. I pumped and wound again. Still it came. Eventually there it was, right in front of me, a huge, swirling, invisible promise in the black water.

I unshipped the net – too soon, of course. While I had been pumping, the fish had been getting its breath back. Without warning it made another searing run, this time diagonally upstream and towards a raft of tree wreckage under the far bank. I thought the leader must surely part when I tried to stop it, but it didn't; the fish came wallowing back, its great tail just visible breaking the surface (I had now jammed my torch between my teeth, something I resort to in angling emergencies). I was downstream from it now, so I just stood in the way like a tired goalkeeper and let the current carry it into the net.

Up on the bank, the cows watched in a respectful semicircle as I weighed my prize: ten pounds twelve ounces of solid silver.

It was not quite two o'clock. I subsided on to the bank and lay back in the grass just as a shooting star flashed across the zenith. I didn't take too much notice. There didn't seem to be anything left to wish for.

Adapted from an article published in Trout & Salmon, *1998*

CHAPTER 14

A river runs through it, but not on Wednesdays

'A still day in the turning world'

Radio Telefís Éireann news report, 13.11.2001

I was loading the car with fishing tackle ready for Ireland when I heard my friend Will's call from the sitting room. "Take a look at this before you go," he said.

He was sitting on the sofa with a cigarette in one hand and a whisky in the other, watching the lunchtime news. "Don't go near any tall buildings while you're away" he said, and waved me to a chair.

It was Tuesday September 11, 2001. As I sat down to see what was going on, the second plane hit the World Trade Center. Neither of us could think of anything to say that was longer than four letters. Will poured a scotch for me and another for himself and we sat in near silence and watched the horror unfold, trying to help things along with our expletives.

I was meeting Tim for the night ferry from Swansea to Cork, so there wasn't much to be done but get on my way and listen to the news teams on the radio trying to piece together the facts behind the nightmare as I drove.

We had a peaceful crossing. The following morning, as we waited for the instruction to disembark, everyone crowded in front of the high-level TV in the ship's lounge to catch up with overnight developments. Couples held hands, the old as well as the young. There was a party of Americans on the ship, two elderly couples touring Europe together, desperate to find out anything they could about what had happened and to know that the folks back home were safe. One of the women was convinced that her sister in New York must be a casualty, because of some connection with the World Trade Center; she was desperate to get ashore to try to find news of her. I felt a little guilty that all we had to do was find a river and go fishing.

We drove in convoy off the boat, Tim leading (he is partly Irish on his mother's side), and headed for the town where we could buy permits. It was a fine morning with a warm westerly coming off the sea, so we drove fast. We were in Ireland, but we were not yet under its spell, and the process of *détente* was not helped by what we knew was happening three thousand miles to the west. I fiddled with the car radio until I found RTE, and listened to events unfold. The soft Irish voices lent a soothing sensitivity to the coverage, and we stayed tuned in for the rest of our trip.

We found the town we sought, and the tackle shop. The man in charge had a complicated menu of options for us, but stripped of the ifs and maybes they boiled down to two; we could fish the main river, which I will call the Gurgle, where there was a 'fine chance' of a salmon, or we could try its tributary the Gargle, a 'shy little river' where there were plenty of good trout and still a chance of a salmon, and to top it all no one had fished it for weeks. Later I realised that I should have asked *why* no one had fished it for weeks, but there you are.

Some water we would need in the Gurgle, for the fish to move, which would be with us next week for sure, but we were here this week, and not for very much of it, so we decided to hedge our bets and try the Gargle.

He shared out the paperwork; licences, permits, tags for any salmon we might catch, a leaflet about the area; a map. Judging by the care with which he had photocopied and taped the map together, he took his cartography seriously. We could see the original on the wall. It was marked up with little colour-coded symbols to show access points, parking places, boundaries and pools. The colour-coding seemed an excellent idea, though of course it did not work quite so well on the photocopy.

"Now" he said, dropping his voice and beckoning us closer. "This is where you'll be fishing. Devil of a lot of fish coming out of there at the start of the season." He reached over and drew a big, careful, cross on our map. "O'Halloran's. Wonderful pool, awful deep. Tommy McMichael had a sixteen-pounder there in June. Start by the fence at the top and fish down to where the old willow used to be."

There was clearly a lot more advice available, but the day was whizzing by, so we assured him we understood and ran out of the shop and back to the cars.

We drove hell for leather for a dozen miles or so out of

town and then stopped in a layby to see which direction we should have been going in. I got out the photocopied map we had been given and my map of South West Ireland. We checked them both against the national road atlas, and cross-referenced them with the map at the back of the tourist guide. When it comes to maps, I need all the help I can get.

"I think if we just drive on for a bit we might see a sign," said Tim. So we drove on for several more miles (or kilometres, to use the Gaelic term); no signs.

Then, without warning, Tim did a J-turn and disappeared up a leafy side road, and I followed on smoking tyres. He had spotted a bridge, and guessed that there would be a river under it. By the time I drew up behind him he was already putting his rod up.

"Do you reckon this is the Gargle?" I said.

"Oh, it will be for sure," said Tim, who had by now become roughly half-Irish. I looked over the bridge, and spotted the river almost immediately. It wasn't terribly wide and a bit shallow into the bargain, and the water in it was not moving all that much (well, not at all in fact) but it looked very nice just the same.

I looked at the tackle dealer's map again. Several road bridges were shown, but there was no clue as to whether ours might be one of them. The river we sought was indicated by a wavy black line. The main road we had just left was indicated by a slightly less wavy black line, and the lane we had turned into by a black line of intermediate waviness. There were lots of other lines on the map, all black of course, some of them almost straight, some crooked and disjointed, some single, some double, many so fine that they had been partly extinguished by the photocopying process. Apart from the lines, however, there wasn't very much else on the map at all. There were a few names; Shaughnessy's, Kilmartin's, O'Neal's. They sounded like bars, but even in Ireland this seemed unlikely, given that there wasn't a town for twenty miles.

Tim rotated the map this way and that, like someone positioning an indoor TV aerial, until he had found our bearings. We were not on the actual Gargle, he pronounced finally, but on one of its tributaries. Well, that was a relief. Pretty as this stream was, it was not really the sort of place I had come to associate with salmon. Even a very small grilse with agoraphobia would have found it a little snug.

After much further study and calculation, we decided that the real Gargle and the pool with the cross would be found at a point two inches sou' sou' west of the bridge; I made that a mile, or possibly only half a mile, or possibly two miles. Or kilometres.

"OK" I said. "Go for it." We went for it. We shouldered our tackle and set off through the undergrowth.

We hadn't been walking for more than an hour or so when Tim dumped his kit in the grass and dug out the map. I waited expectantly. He shouldered his gear again, wiped his brow and struck off to the right, towards a line of trees. "Willows" he said. "Water."

We reached the willows, and stopped. Not that we had to; we could have carried right on walking, because there was absolutely nothing blocking our path, certainly nothing liquid. Just a bit of a depression where a very small ditch might once have been.

A river runs through it, but not on Wednesdays.

We sat down in the grass, panting. I looked at the map again, determined to do the job properly. I looked at the horizon and studied the distribution of woodland and pasture, then compared it with the clues to topography that the map gave us. It didn't take long; there weren't any.

Then I noticed a peculiar thing.

"There's something wrong with the sun," I said to Tim.

"Looks fine to me" he said, in between gasps.

"Ireland isn't in the southern hemisphere, is it? Because unless it is, the sun should be in the south, and it seems to be in the north."

"How foolish we have been" said Tim, after a suitable pause, only he didn't put it quite like that.

I looked around for the embodiment of a cartographic symbol to help us; a triangulation point, an obelisk, perhaps even a Roman villa. I could not see one. We were standing at the edge of a field. To our left and right there were other fields. The fields were separated by hedges or, in some cases, fences. There were cows in some of the fields. The cows were black and white. Need I go on?

We trudged silently back to the cars, climbed in and drove back up to the main road and towards the turning we should have taken. It was a glorious day, with Ireland still swathed in the green of summer, fleecy puffs of cloud rolling by overhead and the road swinging up and down, right and left through gentle valleys and over grassy hills.

On the far side of the Atlantic, under an equally beautiful early autumn sky, they were revising the numbers of dead upwards.

Eventually we found the Gurgle. It was a lovely river, but

it looked much too low to offer the slightest chance of salmon or sea trout. Brown trout would have done us almost equally well, but there was not the slightest sign of them either. We fished until late evening without turning a fin.

The following day we turned to the second stage of our plan; fly-fishing for bass. Tim had realised how well the south-western corner of Ireland is designed for this. It is constructed of low fingers of Devonian sandstone, all pointing west-south-west into the Atlantic. Rather than sheer cliffs, there are endless sprawling promontories which give access to an infinity of little bays and weedy reefs and gullies. We found an enticing spot called Galley Cove, near Crookhaven. The day was bright, the sun was high and the water was as clear as a nun's conscience, so I tackled up well back from the water's edge, then crept forward... but I was not careful enough. Right in front of me in no more than two feet of water was a group of three medium-sized bass. They saw me as I saw them, and darted off like silver bullets before I could unship my fly. We spent the afternoon casting our flies into those clear and lovely waters, without a trace of bass or anything else.

The following day a stiff northerly had blown up, so we took refuge in a sheltered cove somewhere near Crookhaven. It was far too rough for the fly, so I rigged up a spinning rod instead. Unbelievably, at the very first cast the rod hooped round and I felt a lively weight. I pumped, and up came, even more unbelievably, another bass. But it was never going to be so easy. The fish held on until it was happy that I had identified it, then let go.

The second cast brought an even bigger thump, following by a determined plunge for the deeps, but it was not a bass this time. The coppery glint in the water as I pumped the fish up told me that I had hooked a pollack. Nothing like so desirable a quarry, but still great sport. We caught several; the biggest, which I think weighed four and a half pounds, fell to Tim's rod.

On our last day, the Friday, all the shops were closed, so we couldn't buy bait as planned. This was not something we felt inclined to complain about, even to each other, given that they were closed because it had been declared an international day of mourning for the people who had been blasted out of existence in New York. "A still day in the turning world", as the man on RTE put it.

Tim decided to persevere in his quest for bass, while I returned to the river, just in case. I plodded across cornfields and waded through bogs and backwaters until, in the heat of the afternoon, I came to a deep bend of the Gurgle, under some willows. I threaded the line, looking forward to the swish of fly tackle again, though without much hope; the time, the weather and the season were all against me.

But then a fish jumped right in front of me; and another; and another. I had stumbled upon a shoal of sea trout. There must have been a hundred or more of them, all packed into a twenty-yard stretch of deep, silent water under a steep bank studded with the holes of sand martins. I could not see below the surface from the shallow beach on my side of the water, so I watched the jumping for a while to work out what I was up against. There seemed to be fish of all sizes, from half-pound whitling to big ones of four or five pounds. Most of them bore the pewter sheen of fish which have been in the river for a few weeks. It looked a hopeless mission, but an interesting one.

I tried to phone Tim, but there was no signal, so I resolved to do all I could to extract one of these fish and take it back to show him. I had plenty of time before the rendezvous we had arranged that evening at the pub.

It is one of the most optimistic challenges in angling to try to catch clear-water sea trout by day, in bright sunshine, from a shoal of fish which have long since run up from the sea and abandoned any interest in feeding. Your only hope is that the competitive instinct will nudge one of the fish into taking your fly just to stop the next fella getting it. I started with a dry fly on a 4lb point; an olive pattern, I think. One of the smaller fish splashed at it immediately, but after that it was as if a signal had been circulated to the rest of the shoal; *angler in the swim boys, button your lips.*

I waited for everything to calm down, and tried showing them a bushy dry fly; nothing. Then I put up an intermediate line, tied on a size 12 Teal, Blue and Silver (a great attractor of sea trout), cast it quietly in right at the top of the pool and let it work slowly round. Still no response.

Every few minutes, another fish would jump. I noticed that the biggest ones seemed to be concentrated towards the tail of the pool, where the river ran into a little grove of willows. I decided to concentrate on them.

I tried muted shrimp patterns, gaudy lures, wake flies, Medicines, tandems, emergers and goldhead nymphs. I fished them high and fast, and I fished them low and slow. Nothing. It became increasingly clear that these fish knew exactly what was going on and had no intention of taking any fly whatsoever.

Riffling through the box as teatime approached, I came to a particularly tiny wet fly; a Bloody Butcher in about size 16.

I tied it on to a 2½ pound point, degreased the leader with mud and cast the fly out with a sharp flick so that it would cut through the surface and begin to sink before drag could pull on the leader (it works a treat for rainbows on difficult stillwaters).

The leader vanished in an instant and the rod hooped round. I pulled as hard as I dared on the ultra-fine nylon, and a good sea trout pulled right back.

I managed to slow the fish's first rush and to start working it gently back, although I don't think it had really woken up yet to what was happening. Then, just as I was beginning to imagine Tim's face when he saw me walk into the pub with a five-pound sea trout slung over my shoulder, it threw the hook.

That was it. We drove back the next morning to catch the ferry home. On the boat I dug out the map and tried to show Tim where I had encountered that tantalising shoal, but try as I might, I couldn't find a spot that matched my recollections of the place.

When I got home, an information pack was waiting for a fishery in Wales. Among the items was a map of the beat. It was not a reduced photocopy of a local authority plan; it was a colour map, drawn by an artist, of the river. It showed the access points in relation to the neighbouring roads, which were all numbered, and gave an indication of distance. It named the main farms. It indicated the position, size and shape of the car parks. A dotted line showed the paths from the car parks to the water. Best of all, the main features of the river itself were shown, as well as of course the pool names. It did not actually show the fish, but I suppose there has to be some element of challenge.

If only all fishery owners and managers would get someone to do a proper map like that for them. It would prevent unintentional straying on to your neighbour's water (my car was once locked in a field beside the Usk by a farmer who could see me, lacking the help of an anglers' map, unwittingly poaching his water and thought a few hours' detention would teach me a lesson). The map should refer to features that can be recognised by the newcomer, not just those which are meaningful only to people who have lived there since before the Industrial Revolution. And there's no need to show the fish – except on my copy, of course.

Adapted from an article published in Trout and Salmon, *2002*

CHAPTER 15

Of wheels and water

The fog comes on little cat feet...

Carl Sandburg, 'Fog'

A ngling literature, on the whole, disregards the motor car upon which most of us depend for our fishing. Stories of great carp and magical days by distant lochs fail to mention the humdrum details of the transport arrangements. If a vehicle is referred to at all it is dismissed as a sordid necessity, undeserving of a mention in the credits despite its indispensable role in our pleasure.

I have never seen it that way myself. For all their unpopularity in these days of sustainability and carbon footprints, I like cars, and love taking them fishing. One has been my companion on pretty much every outing since the end of my teens; presumably the same applies to you. The good ones have added to the experience, whooshing me and my kit pleasurably down motorways and threading us considerately across boggy pastures and down muddy lanes that are very nearly 'too thin' for a car, as my small daughter once put it. Even the unsuitable ones I've owned (I don't recommend a lowered MGB roadster, or an Austin Maestro with Friday-afternoon electronics) have usually got me there and back again safely, though it doesn't help the enjoyment of a fishing trip when you have to keep wondering if, come nightfall, the car will still be where you left it or have burst the bonds of a dicey handbrake and rolled suicidally into a ditch.

Many of the best vignettes from the fishing trips of memory are set beside cars, or under their raised tailgates. What could be happier than to sit on the luggage lip, sipping from a flask of coffee, tying up leaders and swapping stories with one's fellow anglers? And what quiet joy there is in a languid picnic beside the car in a riverside meadow as you wait for a rise, or the advent of cloud cover.

On a wild, wet day, few places can segregate you more effectively from the rest of the human race than the inside of your car, particularly if you have parked it in an isolated spot beside a wild river or overlooking a bleak foreshore. Snug in your den of metal and glass, rain thudding comfortably on to the roof, you can eat and drink and snooze, read, study, plan, calculate, daydream, even tie flies, in hermit-like peace and seclusion.

Such escapism is, of course, only possible if your car is allowed to accompany you to the waterside. Arriving to find your venue has no parking is about as much fun as finding it has no fish. On one trout stream I know, the only possible parking spots are along a suburban street a couple of hundred yards from the water. You can forget all those fond ideas of tackling up in a lush waterside meadow, then ambling back to the car periodically to put up another rod or sit on the tailgate with a beer and a ham roll. On arrival, the essentially private business of dressing for aquatic combat, threading lines through rings and choosing flies and lures has to be carried out at the kerbside in full view of curious, even hostile, residents, with cars and vans squeezing by every few minutes and threatening to sweep bits of your tackle away with them.

How much more intimate the relationship between a fisherman and his car, and how much more critical the need for solitude, space and greensward, when it becomes his bedroom as well as his base, as mine regularly have for the past thirty-odd years. In my early sea-trouting days in South Wales, struggling to squeeze in as much fishing time as possible between days at work, I would fish until two or three in the morning and then attempt to drive home. Somewhere between Bridgend and Newport, however much coffee I had drunk, my eyelids would start to drift towards my knees. Soon, brief but terrifying moments of unconsciousness would force me to pull into the next services for a half-hour nap, from which I would wake disoriented, cold, stiff and still unpleasantly tired.

These days, night-fishing trips are much more civilised. When the sky has begun to pale and sport is over for the night I simply plod back to the car, take down my rods, swap my waders for my sleeping bag, winch the passenger seat-back all the way down to the horizontal and assume the prone position. Unless an early-morning tractor wakes me I can usually count on sleeping like a baby for around five hours, after which I splash myself awake, tidy up my tackle and drive home, stopping for a café breakfast en route. Or go fishing again, of course.

Pretty much any sizeable modern car will look after a sleeping angler in comfort, though estates are naturally the most practical and four-wheel-drive estates the best of all – fast, streamlined and responsive on the open road, yet capable of negotiating muddy fields and awkward slopes in most weathers. On many fisheries four-wheel drive is unnecessary, but on some it can make the difference between enjoying your car's companionship by the water and leaving it miles away in public view on the side of a main road.

Long experience in this game has taught me a few dodges. Make sure your car has a passenger seat which reclines to the horizontal, or very nearly (the Subarus, Audis, Volvos and BMWs I've driven over the past three decades have all satisfied this requirement very well). You'll need two pillows (one for your head, the other to pad the hollow where the seat joins the seat back) plus one sleeping bag to sleep in and another to act as a mattress. Position the car as far from roads and buildings as you can and preferably away from even the most disused-looking farm track (more than once I have picked an apparently neglected trackway, only to be woken at six by the thunder of farm machinery inches from my ear). Work out where the sun will rise in the morning and park so that there will be trees or a tall hedge between it and you, so you don't start to cook when dawn comes up. If there's a slope, face the car uphill to tilt your bed a little nearer to the horizontal. If you can't find a suitable site close to your fishing spot, be prepared to drive a short distance to one when fishing has finished.

On a dry night it's a simple matter to step out of your

waders and totter round from boot to passenger seat in your socks. I suggest you keep your shoes in the footwell, so you can answer the morning call of nature without getting your feet soaked by the dew (it is just about possible to do this without stepping out of the car, though the less agile may find the necessary contortions beyond them). A rubber mat is useful to stand on while changing foot and legwear, whether you are sleeping in the car or not, but try not to leave it behind when you go, as I have done more than once.

In high summer you might consider carrying a couple of towels to drape over the windows to reduce the impact of the morning sun on your slumbers; alternatively, have a soft hat ready to put over your face when you feel the intrusion of the morning rays.

Never, under any circumstances, even think of doubling up with another angler for a night in your car, however fond you are of each other. By all means share a twin room at the pub if you're too mean to pay for a couple of singles, but do not entertain the idea of sleeping in the same vehicle. Better to doze on a car rug under the stars, with dew on your eyelashes and earwigs in your hair, than endure someone else's creaks, grunts and smells from six inches away, or inflict yours on him.

What to do with the fish you've killed, if any? Before I invested in an insulated fish bag with ice packs, I would hang mine in the fish bass on a shaded tree branch (not over the wing mirror – slime can damage paintwork). If you put a wet fish bass in the car it will stink by morning, and if you leave your catch in the grass you are likely to lose it to a farm cat, a fox or even an otter. You can also buy ice boxes that plug into your car's electrics.

A word of warning about immobilisers and remote controls. One rainy night I returned to my car to find that the keys had got wet in my trouser pocket and the remote no longer worked. I had to open the door with the key, setting off the alarm, and spend the entire night with the dashboard lights flashing in my eyes like a video of Las Vegas. In the morning the remote had dried out and the car and I were back in business, but in wet weather I now tend to remove the battery (in case I press the button without thinking) and operate by key only. Sometimes I don't take the keys away at all, but conceal them in a dry place near the car.

I know many men who switch off their mobile phones on fishing trips, or curse them for tying them to home and work. On the contrary, I have found the cellphone a great aid to fishing. As long as mine remains silent, I know that no crisis has developed back home and that no client or business associate (or wife or offspring) is furiously trying to get in touch. If calls have to be made that could not be made yesterday and cannot wait until tomorrow, I know I can take care of them at or near the waterside instead of having to delay my departure for the river until the business is resolved, or rush home early. A sleeping phone is my assurance that all's well with the world outside; and of course it is there when I need it to call the weather forecast, the automated river-level gauge, the fishery manager or home.

The best phone for a fishing trip has good reception, but lousy sound quality. With my last phone I could speak to clients with a clear conscience even when I was standing waist-deep in a salmon river, but the little devil I have now transmits the sound of running water with Sensurround clarity, necessitating a fifty-yard hike into the backwoods if I wish to lie about my reason for being away from the office.

Whether or not you choose to carry a phone on fishing trips, it is always a comfort to be reunited with the warmth and security of the car after a trying day in wind and rain. Sometimes, it's a bit more than that.

It was the end of summer on the high hills of Powys, the bracken turning to gold and curls of mist collecting in the stream valleys. I had promised myself an afternoon on foot, exploring the upper Elan Valley, so I decided to travel light. I left the car in a rocky alcove somewhere off the road that carries the tourists around the valley on bank holiday weekends like an airport baggage-reclaim conveyor belt and marched down to the lake with just a fly rod and a folding net, my fly box and spare nylon stowed in the pockets of my fishing vest.

As the shadows lengthened towards evening I plodded across the tussocks from promontory to promontory, flushing meadow pipits at every step, to short-line the water across the fading breeze with a team of traditional flies. Nothing doing; too cold and too late in the year, no doubt. I have known some wonderful moments on these upland lakes on a summer's evening, when rising fish would dimple the mirror and come freely to a Black & Peacock Spider, but not today.

If it hadn't been for a single trout which rose solidly in front of me to suggest that the situation might not be hopeless, I would have reeled in around five and wandered comfortably back to the car in time for tea and Welsh cakes back at the vicarage. As it was I decided to fish on a little later; and it wasn't long before I deeply regretted it.

Mist is funny stuff. Sometimes it forms far out across the

water and moves in on you in a pincer movement like the ghost army from *Lord of the Rings*. At other times it rolls down off the hills in clumps like tumbleweed, or sprouts from the hollows and crannies among the turf as if discharged from somewhere deep underground. On this particular evening, it seemed to appear everywhere at once, and I realised with a lurch that I had left my departure stupidly late. I wound in, fastened the tail fly to the keeper ring and swung round to begin the march back, but I hadn't covered twenty yards before the fog rose in my face like a grey wall.

I felt my stomach knot, and tried to tell myself not to let a little water vapour get me rattled, but I knew I had been a fool and would be lucky to get home without trouble. I buttoned my collar, put my head down and continued to march resolutely across the cotton-grass. All I had to do was follow the edge of the lake back the way I had come. Unfortunately, I had been casting and walking for the best part of three hours, so it would be quite a trek.

Imagining that by keeping away from the water I could walk on slightly drier and firmer ground, I began to follow a more inland route; and this was my second mistake. There came a moment, twenty minutes or so into the march, when I realised that I was not walking beside the lake any more. I immediately struck off left to look for it – and found myself going uphill instead of down, which should not have been possible.

I felt the sweat of panic break on my brow, and redoubled my speed. But now, whichever way I turned, I seemed to be heading into the hills, and I knew that once lost in the upland wilderness I would be helpless until morning; and I had no warm clothing, nothing to protect me from a long and bone-chilling night the best part of fifteen hundred feet above sea level.

The light was going, and the wall of mist around me was darkening from light grey to a fathomless blue. I was running out of time. My pace quickened, and pretty soon I was in a muck sweat.

Quite suddenly, the ground disappeared in front of me and I found myself scrabbling for grip on the brink of a ravine. Twenty feet below, I could see a stream rushing between rocks and peat hags; the yellowed bones of a sheep lay across the torrent, its jawbone agape in a ghastly grin. Surely the stream must be heading for the lake, but it was running from right to left, and I had last seen the lake on my right. It didn't make sense. No matter; I was now feeling a desperate need to get off these featureless, terrifying moors and down towards a valley, any valley.

I decided to follow the stream down; everyone knows that's what you do when lost in the hills. I had little hope of ever seeing my car again, but a road or a building of some sort, a house if possible, anything man-made, would be better than this terrifying no man's land.

The stream cascaded down through the rocks for half a mile or so, and I lumbered down after it, stumbling over boulders, until it dropped away into a gorge, lost to sight beneath a screen of hawthorn and mountain ash. I could see no way through.

I sat down on a boulder. I don't remember whether I put my head in my hands, but I think it probable.

And then I heard the most cheering sound imaginable; the

gentle purr of a passing car. Curiously, it seemed to come from almost directly above. I looked up and glimpsed the glow of tail lights disappearing into the fog, and realised that I could see in their aura the outline of something large and rectilinear; the stone parapet of a road bridge. I clambered up the scree and on to the road. I had no idea which road it might be of course, or where it might lead, but it was a proper road which had just been used by a motorist, and that was good enough for me.

Reasoning that the motorist was much more likely to have been heading home from wherever he had been than setting off, I decided to go the same way. It was now pretty close to dark. The roadside was dotted with pale shapes, some of which turned out to be rocks and some roosting sheep; the ones which were sheep identified themselves by raising their heads and bleating half-heartedly as I passed, or scrambling to their feet at the last moment and scurrying to safety. The road wound and undulated as it went, but on the whole it seemed to be leading downhill. After the tussocks and swamps I had been scrambling through, it was like walking on Axminster.

After twenty minutes or so I rounded a bend and there, dripping dew in its alcove, was my car, with an expression on its radiator grille that seemed to be wondering, in a condescending sort of way, what on earth I had been doing all this time.

By the time I got home, I had regained my breath and my composure and my trousers and hair were more or less dry. I walked in and joined the rest of them in front of the television. My wife poured me a glass of claret.

"The lamb needs another half hour," she said. "I didn't think you'd be back just yet."

"No point in fishing late," I replied. "It was getting quite misty up there."

"You don't want to be taking any chances up on those moors at this time of year," said her uncle.

"Absolutely" I said, nodding sagely. "Could you pass the nuts, please?"

CHAPTER 16

Something in silver

Not brainless, puny, darting things
But wise important water-kings
That have no time for hooks and lines…

From 'A Corner of the Meadow', Edmund Blunden

As each season on my river draws to a close I promise myself that next year I'll make an early start, in the hope of getting to grips with one of the great sea trout that run the Towy in April and May; although there are big fish to be had all through the season, the average weight is particularly high in the early months, with a real chance of a double-figure fish. But each year, spring manages to arrive in an unexpected rush. By the time I've torn myself away from work and family, precious weeks have already zipped past.

It doesn't help that though these spring sewin are alluringly large – six and seven-pounders are nothing to shout about – I also know you don't run into them every day. And it's a long drive just to stand in the water and soak up the scenery, when the angling urge still hasn't fully emerged from hibernation and the garden is doing its best to return to primaeval forest.

But the 2004 season began with a good spate. And when the May sun comes laughing over the garden fence and the information line tells you the river is at just the right height, you know that the moment has come for you to fire up your hunting genes and pull out your rods and waders.

By the weekend it looked as if the river would be dropping nicely, so I fixed my trip for the Sunday, May 9. Knowing a blank day was much the likeliest outcome, I didn't toss and turn on the Saturday night as I do during the overnight campaigns of high summer; I slept through to the alarm at 4.45. Then I pointed the car west, stopped at Pont Abraham for breakfast and at eight o'clock sharp I was leaning over Golden Grove Bridge. The banks were clad in the freshest spring green and the water looked to be a foot and a half up, coloured, but clear enough for the bottom to show in the shallower margins – just about perfect, in fact.

I sat on a boulder and paid my respects to the river as I do at the start of each season; an old friend revisited after an unduly long absence. Nice to be back. How's it been, winter floods go OK? Hey, you've made a nice job of that shingle bank, just what the pool needed. No no, I wasn't expecting a fish or anything, just dropping by for a few practice casts – but there again, if you *did* happen to have something in silver…

I put up my 13ft double-hander, with a tube fly on a sinking line – with the river slowly easing down I thought it might be worth a cast or two, and no one but a madman or a zombie can spin all day – but the initial casts confirmed that it was all just a bit too big and fast for the fly, so I turned to my spinning rod with a small black-and-silver flying C tied below a ball-bearing swivel, with the aim of switching back to the fly as soon as the water had dropped a little.

I began quietly to fish, wading and casting and retrieving and drinking in the glint and gurgle of the water and noting how the pools and banks had changed over the winter. No pressure to find any actual fish; certainly no worries about failing in the midst of plenty, because there was no plenty, nor would there be for a few weeks yet.

I worked my way down though the Poplars and on towards the Bridge without a sign of a fish, or indeed of a fisherman, which was not surprising this early in the season. To be out on the river again after the long winter, that was the thing. By June the water would have dropped and the river would be shimmering with sewin. Then my hunter's blood would be coursing, but for now, just to be there was enough.

The river and the morning slid peacefully by, interrupted only by cars stopping periodically behind the parapet of the bridge while their owners' heads bobbed up and down like shooting-gallery targets to inspect the water. Sand martins swerved and banked after the sparse early olive hatches and dippers and kingfishers arrowed up and down the straights, but that was all the excitement there was.

At midday I wound in and drove round to Pentrecwn Farm, which gives access to the upper part of the beat. Here, out of earshot of the road, the Towy winds in lazy loops across undisturbed pastures, with only the battlements of Dynevor Castle puncturing the skyline. I gave it a few casts each in the

Whistle Pool and along the Flats, then worked my way more carefully down through the Groynes, which is full of deep, fishy corners. Fishy in high summer, that is – on this early May day they didn't seem much more than nice places to test a lure.

The day was warming now; one or two orange-tips were beginning to plod past in the pale spring sun and a tortoiseshell basked on a piece of driftwood. I pulled off my coat and dropped it on the shingle.

The next stop down is a typical Towy corner pool, a long, narrow stretch of fast, gravelly water which curves around a shingle promontory before opening out into a deep holding pool called the Wall. There is a good taking spot at the top, just where the current slants across a gravel spit and rolls over into the green depths of the pool. I started to fish more searchingly, just in case; full concentration now, with only half a pace between casts.

And it was here, entirely without warning, as the lure swung round into the throat of the pool, that something sandbagged my rod and pulled it round into an angry black hoop.

As I said, you don't find small fish in the Towy in May, so there was nothing initially shocking about this one's determination to stay in the river. I fumbled at the reel check to try to stop the fish reaching the flood wreckage under the far bank. The pressure grew and the rod bent round even further, and then the fish jumped in the centre of the pool, heavy and silver and beautiful, and I knew it was a real cracker of a sewin, surely into double figures. It was bigger than anything I'd had the previous year, that's for sure. In a rush that old feeling was back; the dry mouth, the tight stomach, the shaking knee, the strange sense that all this was happening to someone else.

The fish jumped again, nearer, and it looked bigger – definitely well into double figures. Please let it stay on, I muttered, please let it not find a snag. I looked around for a witness, hoping to see one of my fellow rods jogging up the field to share in the excitement, but there were only the cows and the plodding orange-tips.

Three or four more times I pumped the fish in close and then had to grapple with the reel as the rod bucked to another mighty plunge and the sewin charged away again across the pool. But time and space were on my side, and at last the rushes stopped and a great silver flank swung up and into the bank. Trying to keep an even tension on the line with my rod hand, I unshipped the net and drew the fish gingerly towards it.

My twenty-inch Whitlock has detained many a sea trout and grilse without turning a hair. But as fish and mesh coincided in the slack water, I did a double take. For an instant I thought I'd brought my trout net by mistake. The Whitlock was dwarfed by the fish; eclipsed by it.

I fed the creature nose-first into the mesh, then dragged the whole shooting match ashore as best I could, laid the fish disbelievingly on the grass and knelt before it, wildly surmising what its weight might be; there was nothing to go on apart from the fact that it made my tackle, me and everything around us seem so laughably small. I fumbled for the 11lb spring balance I usually carry in my shoulder bag, but it wasn't there and I didn't think it would be up to this fish anyway, so I left my tackle in the grass, wrapped the fish in my salmon bass, clutched the parcel in my arms like a sick child and half-ran back across the fields to the farmyard.

Back at the car, the truth. Seventeen pounds four ounces

of fresh-run cock Towy sewin; thirty-four inches of solid silver. Utterly astonishing, and with the very first take of the season.

I took a couple of photographs, to prove to myself as much as to anyone else that the fish was real, then slid it carefully into a jumbo-sized fish bag and broached a celebratory bottle of ginger beer. Then I phoned Ian, the fishery manager, to tell him what had happened; he was on his boat somewhere out in Carmarthen Bay, so with the noise of the wind and the boat's engine he had to ask me to repeat the story a couple of times. It would be the biggest fish from the river for the past two seasons, he thought. Ian's wife Rose kindly offered to accommodate the fish in their freezer, to keep it perfect while I fished on. I knew that if ever in my life I were to have a fish mounted, this would be the one.

At the cottage Rose and I laid the fish out, and she made me a cup of coffee. She has seen a lot of sewin, but even she was impressed by this one.

It was some time before I got back to the river, retrieved my tackle and cast out again, and on the very first cast, in exactly the same spot, I took a bright six-pounder. I held it in the mesh, eased out the hook, pointed the fish's nose into the current and let go. After what had happened, killing it would have been sheer greed, yet I found myself fishing on with a most peculiar sense of unease. For years in the 1980s I had lain awake at night plotting battles with six-pound sea trout; now I was shaking them off and sending them away to grow bigger. In the seventies, I had lost my hunger for tench and pike. In the eighties, the reservoir rainbows had gone the same way. The notion that my passion for sea trout might also fade filled me with a kind of subdued panic.

In the late afternoon I packed up, collected my fish from Rose and drove homeward via Nantgaredig Bridge, the place where nearly twenty years earlier I had first looked upon the waters of the Towy. Cyril the gillie was there, and so was Ian, who had stopped to look at the river on his way back from the boat. I showed them the shining slab that lay across the boot of my car, and they said very little, except that they thought it would have a good chance of being the biggest sewin from the Towy that season.

When they had gone, I walked to the centre of the bridge and took in the familiar scene. A hundred times I had gazed into this pool, longing to know its secrets. Now they scarcely mattered. What could it hold that would not be trumped by the thing in the boot of my car? The Towy does occasionally produce bigger sewin, but not by much.

I knew I hadn't really deserved the fish; that a specimen high-water sea trout on spinning tackle is not a reward for angling skill but a lottery win, a lucky accident waiting to happen. I could claim credit for managing to keep my head after the fish took, but that was about it.

Not that this deterred me from having the fish professionally set up. After it had spent some years looking down at me from the wall of my sitting room, the fishery owner, Sir Edward Dashwood, made me a generous offer for it and it is now on view to visiting anglers in the residential fishing lodge at Abercothi.

So what do you do when you've achieved a dream? How can a man go on fantasizing about leviathans when he has already taken a fish like that, a sea trout in ten thousand, even by Towy standards?

What I needed after that, of course, was a string of blanks to push the world back into perspective and reawaken the old hunger. And that's exactly what I got. It wasn't until early July that I managed to get another decent sewin, on the fly this time. And, thank goodness, the stomach tightened, the hand shook and the knee trembled, just as they had in the good old days.

Normal service had been resumed.

CHAPTER 17

In search of Hugh

What do men do with their stolen time? Everyone lives in the tight little house of his mind, each with its own façade, and no one really knows what goes on in the next house.

Hugh Falkus, 'The Stolen Years'

D o you remember what you were doing in late February 1976? It may help to recall that Concorde had just started taking passengers, Britain and Iceland were in the process of breaking off diplomatic relations over the 'cod wars' and Abba's *Mamma Mia* had just managed to topple Queen's *Bohemian Rhapsody* from the top of the pop charts.

At 7.25 pm on the evening of Sunday February 22nd that year, BBC2 broadcast a programme which changed me a little for ever. If you're an angler of a certain age, it may have done the same for you. The latest in the much-loved *World About*

Us series, it was entitled *Self Portrait Of A Happy Man*, and the writer, narrator and subject were the same person – Hugh Falkus. I watched in awe as that rugged, windswept figure in his Solway zipper, a brace of Labradors obedient at his heel, strode out past a vista of Lakeland peaks to the banks of the most beautiful stretch of water I had ever seen – which he introduced as *his* river. I saw how cheerfully his delightful wife Kathleen attended to the kitchen and vegetable garden while Hugh concentrated on the much more important business of tying flies for sea trout. I watched on the edge of my chair as he cast one of them into the darkness of a Cumbrian summer night, and cheered with excitement as, after a thrilling battle, he netted a fresh-run six-pounder.

Hugh told us how he made his living from writing books and making films about fishing and the countryside (I was halfway through a brief stint as an information officer with the Central Office of Information at the time, and I would have given all my possessions to trade that job for a chance to get paid for writing about the wild). He showed us some of the wildlife that shared his valley, and took us out on the ocean in a proper fishing boat. Was there nothing about this man's life that was not perfect?

Of course, there was a great deal about Hugh Falkus' life that was not perfect. As the years went by and I became involved in game fishing, I began to realise, from hints in press articles and the talk of fellow anglers who knew something of the man, that behind the charismatic angler, game shot, naturalist, writer, outdoorsman, sailor, broadcaster, teacher, showman, entertainer and hellraiser lay a deeply-troubled soul.

I learned early on from press articles that Hugh had flown

a Spitfire in World War II, shot down some enemy bombers and endured the horrors of prison camp; naturally this only strengthened his image. The news that after the war his courage and athleticism had enabled him to survive a boating accident which had claimed the lives of his new young wife and three friends deserved sympathy, even admiration. But then it appeared that Hugh's darker episodes had not been confined to the outdoors; between the tussles and triumphs of which he liked to speak, some of the less edifying pages in Hugh's photo album seemed to have been torn out. There had been two additional marriages, both of which had crashed in ruins, while somewhere along the line Hugh had managed to father and forget two, three or possibly four children, depending on who you asked about it.

Then in the mid-1980s, as mentioned earlier, I bought *Sea Trout Fishing: A Guide To Success*, and Hugh became my angling mentor and inspiration. How that green bible fired my heart! Not since childhood, when a kind uncle had given me Bernard Venables' *Mr Crabtree Goes Fishing*, had an angling book so captured my imagination. Hugh drove me to the river, and in the late 1980s and early 1990s I did the same for him, a hundred times over. Many a night I would retire to the car in the early hours cold, tired and dispirited, drag off my waders and turn to Hugh for solace before turning in. I would read a couple of pages of 'Night Fly Fishing Strategy – The Approach' or 'Part Three – Sunk Line' – and magically the dismay and the defeat would drop away and I would find myself once more booted and spurred and striding back to the fray.

"Nothing must be allowed to undermine your confidence, for nothing can be done on the river without it," wrote Hugh.

The extra dose of determination his words gave me brought memorable moments of triumph to quite a few apparently hopeless outings.

Late one misty night in July 1994, I took a couple of big fish directly as a result of Hugh's advice. The following day, unable to concentrate on work, I decided to pen a short thank-you letter to the man himself. I did not expect him to stoop to a reply, but barely 36 hours later the postman delivered a slim grey-green envelope with a little gold sticker on the flap imprinted with the great man's name and address. Inside was a plain white postcard covered on both sides with exuberant handwriting.

"Thank you for your interesting letter" it said. "I'm delighted at your success. Persist with the sunk lure – it is far and away the best 'fly' for catching sea-trout late at night, fished deep on a sunk line. _But_ if you are not giving the surface lure a try as well, you are depriving yourself of some dramatic moments. _Always_ give it a try – as described in my book."

A few nights later I was back at the water to do Hugh's bidding. I had armed myself with a selection of home-made surface lures and planned to follow his instructions, grass a decent sewin or two and write again to tell him about it, perhaps raising one or two intriguing questions of lure presentation or sea-trout biology. So would begin a long correspondence between master and pupil which at the very least would make me the envy of my less exalted fishing buddies.

Hugh's magic worked, in spectacular fashion. The very first time I cast one of these lures on to the inky surface of one of my favourite Towy pools it was seized with great violence. Unfortunately the fish let go again very nearly as quickly, and although there were other expressions of interest, none was as decisive as the first, and I did not hook another fish. In the end I went back to the sunk fly, thinking I would try again next week.

But then the rains came, then it was autumn, and then it was 1995, a much less rewarding season, with few opportunities to fish. I managed to take only a handful of small sea-trout, none of them on a surface lure. My return letter to Hugh remained on ice. Then one April morning in 1996 I spread the daily paper out on the kitchen table and saw his name spread across the obituary pages; he had died, of cancer, just short of his 79th birthday.

I was still annoyed with Dick Walker for leaving us so prematurely in 1985, and I had yet to come to terms with the loss of BB in 1990; I had written him a letter too, with some news about purple emperor butterflies, a great passion of his, but hadn't got round to posting it. I hadn't known Hugh was ill; I knew he couldn't live for ever but had hoped he would at least match his father, who, as he so movingly related in *The Stolen Years* (which is quite possibly the best book mainly about angling ever written) lived to the grand old age of eighty-five.

I waited nine years for Hugh's biography before I realised that I was going to have to write it myself.

At first, this was a great puzzle to me. Surely any writer – particularly any angling writer – would jump at the chance to explore such a colourful and enigmatic life? But I discovered that those who had known Hugh were reluctant to take on his life story because they felt it would amount to disloyalty to a man they had counted a friend. Professional writers who had not known Hugh so well, but were qualified to tackle the job, understood more than I did then about the economics of writing and publishing and the likely small return from such a book.

So it became a labour of love. Client accounts remained neglected, gardens unweeded, cars unwashed and unserviced and rivers unfished while I applied myself to it. All my old reporters' instincts, all the old persistence and attention to detail, came back as if they had never been forgotten. My hard-earned skills in encouraging people to talk, asking the right questions and persisting (sometimes, by social standards, to the point of rudeness) until I had the information I needed, all returned as if they had never been away.

I could not believe how helpful everyone was. With scarcely an exception, all those I approached – Hugh's family and friends, fellow fishermen, fellow writers and broadcasters, even one or two of the women in his life – gave me their time, invited me into their homes, lent me old papers and photographs and even, in some cases, carried out small chunks of my research for me.

How did it feel to slowly dismember my hero's image, to begin filling in the many gaps he had left in his life story, to unstitch and reweave the somewhat glamorised history he had created for himself? There are those who believe a man's secrets should be allowed to die with him; Charles Jardine, mentioned in an earlier chapter, gave me that view at the launch of the book at the Game Fair. If Hugh's family and friends had felt the same way, I would not have been able to write the book even if I had still wanted to, but they did not. With hardly an exception, they wanted Hugh's story to be told in full. His friends and supporters were keen to see his remarkable achievements in the worlds of angling, writing and broadcasting mapped out and explained for posterity, but they all agreed that this could not be done without a truthful account of the man's complex personality. His surviving children, Mary and Malcolm, who had known a very different Hugh Falkus, wanted him neither lionised nor bowdlerised. They urged me to write the truth, and promised me – and later delivered – every assistance in doing so.

I reflected that it was just as well I had never attempted to make Hugh's acquaintance during his lifetime. Several of his friends told me that he was capable of being brutally rude, both to his supposed allies and to new people he didn't take to, particularly if they dared to challenge some aspect of his teachings. It wouldn't have been much fun to have the reverence I felt for my hero shredded by a volley of four-letter words.

In piecing together the story of Hugh's life I discovered a good deal else that the world did not know about him, and some things even his closest friends had not suspected. I will never entirely understand what could drive a man to cut himself off from his children, or to behave so cruelly towards some of those who loved and cared for him, but then, I had the comfort of knowing him only from a safe distance. I doubt if I could have celebrated Hugh's achievements as fully if I had been among those who were spurned or insulted by him. On the other hand, I could certainly not have applied the magnifying glass to his private life so dispassionately if I had been one of his 'Trusties'.

I have been asked if Hugh Falkus is still a hero to me. The

man who wrote *Sea Trout Fishing* most certainly is. My copy now bristles with colour-coded Post-It notes as a result of my analysis for the relevant chapters of my book, but I still pick my way round them to read the crucial passages when I am building up to a trip to the river, particularly the first one of the season. Hugh virtually *gave* me the sport, and it is mine for life – as it is for all the thousands of others whom he inspired.

When I knew I was going to be writing his story, I started by driving north to see the valley where it had all happened. At the kind invitation of Kathleen's niece, Jane Charlesworth, I toured Cragg Cottage, now discreetly modernised as a holiday let, though Hugh's famous study has been left intact. When Jane had gone I sat for a long time in the tangled garden, alone on a summer's afternoon while the curlews bubbled on the fells and the rooks squabbled from the spinney behind, and I thought of Arthur Oglesby, Fred Buller, Fred J Taylor, Eric Horsfall-Turner, Michael Hordern, and all the other angling personalities who had clinked glasses, swapped banter and assembled their tackle here in those days so long ago when the Esk had run silver with sea trout and Hugh had ruled the valley.

At dusk I pulled on my boots and put up my rod, just as Hugh himself had done so many times over so many years, and walked down to the river. Although the owner of the rights, Hugh's friend Anthony Desbruslais, had generously invited me to fish Hugh's water, I felt an intruder – and something of an impostor. Hugh himself had not known of my existence, except as the author of a single fan letter. Without his blessing, I somehow felt that I should not have been there. What right did I have to be walking the banks of HIS river like this, pursuing HIS fish, the better to trample on HIS memory? I imagined Hugh's spirit swooping from the fells, ghostly stick in hand, spectral dogs bounding ahead, to drive this cocky intruder from his domain.

But I felt no ghosts by that wild and lovely river, no baleful presences; nothing but the scents and sounds of a perfect upland summer's night, all pretty much as Hugh had promised they would be. I smelled the bog myrtle, saw the otter and heard the tawny owl, and saw Arcturus, the night fisherman's star as he called it, the third brightest star in the northern sky, twinkling overhead. At one heart-stopping moment I felt the sudden violence of a taking sea trout, and as the pale dawn showed over Scafell I managed to grass a small one. It went back, of course.

There followed two and a half fascinating years of research, of interviews, of study of ancient newspaper cuttings and yellowed correspondence. I was helped by all those of Hugh's surviving friends I could reach, without exception; only one person, the woman for whom he had once left Kathleen, understandably declined to speak to me. The celebrated Fred J Taylor, in poor health by then (he died aged 89 in 2008), gave me hours of his time at his home in Aylesbury. The other famous fishing Fred, Fred Buller, did likewise, and took the trouble, as the angling historian he was, to dig out material from his archives for my perusal (Fred also made it to 89, sadly leaving us in 2016). I had further extensive help from David Burnett, Hugh's editor and publisher, Bill Arnold, his great friend and ally in his last years, his friends Mike Daunt, Malcolm Greenhalgh, Anthony Desbruslais, Peter Behan and Tim Thomas, the angling book specialist David Beazley, writers

Sandy Leventon, Crawford Little, David Profumo, Graeme Harris, Moc Morgan and Brian Clarke and from the TV wildlife documentary world, Hugh Maynard, Jeffery Boswall, John Sparks and Mike Kendall, to mention but some of the many who contributed. Many of these men were already well-known figures to me, and I felt I was mixing with royalty, though none of them showed the slightest hint of self-importance. Some of my most helpful and revealing sources were however women; they included Hugh's daughter Mary, now a Benedictine nun, Lady Mairi Bury, daughter of the seventh Marquess of Londonderry and once his sister-in-law, and Toni Richards, with whom he had an affair in Eskdale.

What would Hugh have felt about the book? Inevitably he would not have been pleased by some of the revelations in it, though he must have known that a future biographer would find it easy enough to piece together the true story of his life, as opposed to the rather more glamorous version he liked to put about during his lifetime. Yet I hope he would have forgiven me all that for the detailed chapters about his enormous contributions to fishing, to wildlife film-making and to literature.

More than one of Hugh's friends has told me of his great fear of being forgotten, of his legacy fading and his teachings being superseded. The Welsh sea trout expert Graeme Harris told me that Falkus declined a request to provide the foreword to *Successful Sea Trout Fishing*, the book Harris wrote with the late and much-missed Moc Morgan, because he did not want to be perceived to be handing his mantle on to a successor (Sandy Leventon, then Editor of *Trout & Salmon*, wrote it instead). Harris & Morgan's work is probably the book which has so far come closest to succeeding *Sea Trout Fishing* as a modern bible of the game. He made arrangements for his casting school to be carried on by Mike Daunt after his death, on the understanding that it would continue to be known as the Hugh Falkus School of Speycasting. In short, like many egotistical, high-achieving men, he wanted to be remembered and talked about after his death. I hope, therefore, that if he is looking on from somewhere up there (or from somewhere down there, as more than one of his friends have joked) he will forgive my book.

CHAPTER 18

Season's end

The river's tent is broken: the last fingers of leaf
Clutch and sink into the wet bank. The wind
Crosses the brown land, unheard. The nymphs are departed.
Sweet Thames, run softly, till I end my song.

T S Eliot, 'The Waste Land'

A dark bulge shows itself briefly above the river's surface, and I stop what I am doing and stare. A few seconds later, there it is again a few feet to the left, but now it is clearer. It is not a rolling salmon, as I had thought, but the flat bulge of the head of an otter cruising nostril-deep across the brown waters of the pool I am watching. A moment later the water lies once again in peace, the bankside mist flooding with patches of yellow and gold as an October morning sun begins to light up the thickets of balsam and young willow.

I am slightly relieved that the bulge wasn't a salmon, because all this is happening on a computer screen and in my right hand I am manipulating not a rod but a mouse. I am sitting at my desk a hundred and twenty miles from the river, editing a client's manuscript on one monitor while on the other, courtesy of Abercothi Fishery and Farson Digital Watercams, the real-time image of a famous Towy pool clicks from frame to frame at ten-second intervals.

I click on the 'zoomed image for water levels' tab to check the water height; there's the gauge, palely loitering in its hollow under the bank. It confirms that the river is about fifteen inches above summer low, an excellent height for running salmon. I would give a king's ransom to swap the mouse for the rod, but it is not possible, not this week and probably not next.

A little later, sitting back in my chair with a mid-morning cup of coffee, I click on to the Cothi camera stationed a few hundred yards to the west. Far up at the top of the pool in the distance, I can see a fence post that is too tall for a fence post and realise I am looking at the figure of an angler fishing his way down the Escarpment Pool. I took a nice sea trout from the very spot where he's standing just a few short weeks ago; it was still high summer back then. I can't see his rod at this distance on this grainy image (though I can tell from his stance it's a single-hander), but I know exactly where his fly is working; hard under the steep left bank in a deep, curling run where sewin lie all summer long. The sea trout fishing is over now, so I imagine he is working an Ally's Shrimp or a Munro Killer through on a sunk leader in the hope of a salmon. The shingle bank he's fishing from is fully exposed and in the foreground the camera is showing me stones under the water, so I'm guessing the Cothi might be a little too low and clear for him to have much chance of success.

My matchstick angler jerks downstream from station to station at ten-second intervals as the webcam cycles on, and then suddenly I get a frame in which he has waded on to dry land and is standing on the shingle, glaring at the river with his fists on his hips. I know exactly what that pose means: *damn river, what the heck am I going to do with you?* Shortly after this the camera collects one, two, three frames of him beetling away from the water and up through the gorse, like the drawings of the creature in the M R James ghost story *The Mezzotint*, until finally my riverscape is once again empty of humanity. Nothing doing, obviously. I wish my vanished angler success for the rest of his day, but not too much success, given that I can't share it with him. Perhaps he will appear on the Towy camera at some point, but I might have to wait a while; he has a score of good pools to choose from, and I know them all well.

It's a terrible distraction from work, this webcam game (and not recommended during office hours if you are an employee who could be sacked for virtual truancy), but it does provide a certain comfort when business and family commitments keep you away from your river, rather like skyping a distant loved one. I may return to my lonely window on the water at intervals during the long, bleak months, although by then the action is restricted to cows, sheep, tractors and fleeting images of the larger wildlife, if you persist; a heron, a fox, another otter.

A week or so later, I log in again. Now it's the last day of the season and I can see three people fishing the pool, rather more than it has room for. In one frame I can just see the nearest chap's rod, and it's well bent. Is he playing a fish, or just winding in against the current? He is certainly spinning, because the rain has come at last, in the very last three days, and it's far too high now for the fly. There's another frame in which he is climbing up the bank, and now he is sitting or kneeling down – dealing with a fish? I cannot tell, but I hope so. And so my season ends.

Sometimes on a winter's night, taking the dogs for a bedtime leg-stretcher down the lane below the cottage, I look up at the clouds bowling past the moon and listen to the rushing December wind and imagine that the lane is my river and the oaks and birches on either side are the alders and poplars that line my favourite pool. I pause for a moment in the middle of the lane and pretend I am standing waist-deep in the Towy with my favourite Hardy ten-footer in my right hand and the line cradled in the fingers of my left, waiting as the fly swings round unseen under the shadows. As I feel the line straighten below me I draw it in and drive the rod back, then forward again, letting the line whizz off into the dark. I pause for a moment, waiting for the fly to settle. My fingers remember the draw of the invisible current and just then, though I had not scripted this, my subconscious imagination provides the genuine shock of a take. Damn, missed it!

The dogs watch all this in perplexity. Our spaniel misunderstands entirely, though she's seen it before; she thinks I have been throwing a stick for her, and rushes off into the dark to hunt for it. I put away the imaginary rod and scrape around for a real stick for her and throw that instead. The spell is broken, and I whistle the dogs in and trudge back up to the house.

And so to bed, to dream of another season, of dark nights by far-off rivers, of communion with wild places and wild things, and of those great silver fish smashing the moonlit water to stars…

Tight lines.

Printed in Great Britain
by Amazon